The Pace of a Hen

+ *Those seeking*
the life of the spirit
should be cheerful and free,
and not neglect recreation.

+ *Married people must act*
in conformity with their
vocation—

but their progress
will of necessity be
but the pace of a hen.

—Saint Teresa of Avila

The Pace

of a Hen

JOSEPHINE MOFFETT BENTON

A Christian Education Press Publication

UNITED CHURCH PRESS · PHILADELPHIA and BOSTON

Copyright 1961
THE CHRISTIAN EDUCATION PRESS

Second Printing, December 1961

Third Printing, April 1962

Fourth Printing, October 1962

Fifth Printing, February 1964

Sixth Printing, October 1964

Seventh Printing, February 1966

Eighth Printing, May 1969

Library of Congress Catalog Card Number 61-11487

To
All Who Have Helped
in Ways Many and Various
This Book
Is Lovingly Dedicated

+

Foreword

"CERTAIN AUTHORS," says Pascal, "speaking of their works, say 'My Book.' They would do better to say 'Our Book' because there is in them generally more of other people's than their own."

Truly, this book is not my book but our book. It is the book of my friends, my family, my favorite writers. It is a book which grew out of the Pendle Hill pamphlet *Martha and Mary*, which in its turn grew out of the pooled wisdom of a group of women who sat and talked one sunny autumn afternoon about a woman's relationship to her home and her family, to her work and her spiritual life. We came to see that it was not a matter of choice between the roles of Martha and Mary, but a recognition of the diverse facets of almost every woman's nature.

The reconciliation of a woman's many selves is a slow process. Richard Cabot taught my generation in his book *What Men Live By* that the integrated person, the one who faces reality, is never an extremist but one who keeps his equilibrium. The ever-increasing demands on a modern woman's time and energy, her wide interests, her own high standards of performance, pull her in many directions. Her scattered life does indeed resemble the pace of a hen. For her the golden mean is achieved only as she is able to find her way between work and play, between home and community, between solitude and society, between the wisdom

vii

of the serpent and the gentleness of the dove. But in time, with some years given mainly to the nurture of the family, some years to this field of service or that avocation, these seeming fragments can fit together to make a shining pattern of wholeness.

JOSEPHINE M. BENTON

+

Contents

+

1. *The Pace
    of a Hen*

"THOSE SEEKING the life of the spirit should be cheerful and free, and not neglect recreation. Married people must act in conformity with their vocation—but their progress will of necessity be but the pace of a hen."

Years ago those words of the sixteenth-century Spanish saint, Teresa of Avila, began to give me comfort and hope. Since a married woman's life is always overflowing with things that need doing she seems to have very little time to pause and think of the goodness of God. As to making progress in the life of the spirit, how can she when her days are spent going in circles? And then in my floundering I caught a vision from—of all things—Teresa's lowly hen.

But are we modern women willing to picture ourselves in the ridiculous role of a hen, an old-fashioned hen, to be exact? It is not the caged hen in her modern wire-screened individual compartment house that illustrates the "pace" married women must follow. The clucking hen of yester-year that ran uncertainly back and forth across the highway depicts the progress of most of us. So beset was that unfenced barnyard fowl that she did not appear to go anywhere; certainly she did not have the satisfaction of migrating twice each year, as do the song birds, and yet she brought forth creation of daily usefulness.

1

If the hen's pace as a symbol of a woman's journey seems to mock her dignity, reassurance may be found in recalling other spiritual writers who ennobled the lowly hen. In *Pilgrim's Progress* Bunyan shows Christiana and Mercy a hen and her chicks that they may learn from them to praise and thank God for their blessings. Saint Francis once asked, "What am I?" and then told of a dream in which he had seen himself as a little black hen. "Look at me well," he laughed, "I am that hen, small of stature and black."

We honor and are grateful for those single women down through the ages who by means of rigid, self-imposed discipline have added to the world's healing and holiness, learning and beauty. The great female saints, like the Teresas, deliberately chose to become brides of Christ rather than of men. Their pace was that of the eagle and the dove rather than of the hen. In modern times, there are the Jane Addamses, the Muriel Lesters, the Sister Kenneys.

But most of us have chosen the ordinary way, believing people were made to live two by two. A man usually decides on a career, and then takes to himself a wife. It is not that his family is unimportant, but that his field of work is his driving interest. A woman wants above all to have a husband and children. She may be trained as doctor or teacher; she may have a talent for music or the stage; but basically her urge is to create a family and to love and care for them. She must walk a precarious way between her family, her work, her desire to be of service in the community, and her need for recreation and worship.

Her scattered life looks as if she were going around in circles. And why not? What other way is there to go, ultimately? The longest trip that we can set out upon (until we learn our way in outer space) is to go around the world. And in time, we go around the year—spring, summer, autumn, winter. Within that larger cycle of time is the daily one—early morning, high noon, sundown, night. Each new day can bring redemption for us, even as each springtime brings renewal for tree and flower and grass.

Old earth is a sphere that travels around the sun, as the moon in its orbit travels around our earth. The very course of blood through our veins and arteries is known as the circulatory system. The emblem of divinity is a halo. Why disparage going around in circles? Any other route suggests imbalance, a jumping-off-place, abyss. Perhaps the hen's pace is a wholesome one in rhythm with the universe.

WIFE'S OCCUPATION

At the risk of sounding woefully old-fashioned, I must say that I still believe the earning of the family livelihood belongs largely in the hands of the husband. The success of some exceptional couples seems to challenge this statement. Perhaps young wives may work without harmful effects if childbearing is not postponed indefinitely. Once there are children, it is essential to the well-being of preschoolers that their mothers be at home. A social worker urged me to say this in loud tones.

The experts on juvenile delinquency and problem children agree that no substitute takes the place of mother during the early years. But they say that older children suffer no ill effects if their mothers work only during school hours. (Of course these authorities maintain that such women must be stable and competent to keep the relationship with their children on a high level.) Can a job be found that enables a mother to be at home to greet her returning children? The anthropologist, Margaret Mead, says that one of the most disruptive influences in modern life results from the lack of a maternal voice waiting to say, "Johnny, where on earth have you been?"

It seems to me, though, that there is no need for a woman

to be pulled out of the framework of the home in order to fulfill her desire to make a creative contribution to life. I am always hopeful that the pendulum will swing back and that women will see again not only the necessity of a mother's being at home, but also the infinite and rich choice in that occupation for women of all ages. Some will complain of monotony, but how few going out to a paid job have the opportunity to make their own schedules, to choose the routine of their week's labor, to follow up creative interests that women have within the home. Our ever-present disciplines, the pattern of creaturely necessities—cooking, laundry, decently clean houses—are a blessing. Beyond the physical care of the family, for better or worse we are shaping souls and characters. Women learn slowly the magnitude of their influence. Perhaps we would be more contented if we could realize that one of the few remaining free professions is that of housewife. If a woman resents being just a housewife, let her be called an artist, for the dictionary definition of that word is "one who works artistically"; furthermore, "the work of the artist is creative."

Nevertheless, instead of seeing this hard-working span of years as a time of disciplined growth, it is too commonly thought of as a time of intellectual stagnation for the young mother. Perhaps it is the rhythm of nature for her to be somewhat dormant during the nesting years, and right for her to take a vacation from solving the problems of the world. We let land lie fallow that it may later produce a more abundant harvest. After her dormant and fallow, yet creatively constructive, years she may arise to have some vision toward the solutions of racial tension, strikes, starvation, and nuclear warfare. A mother is the ground from which hope springs.

Really they are not dormant years with nothing happening to stimulate a housebound woman's mental processes, any more than nothing is happening in the fallow field where bacteria, molds, earthworms, and weeds are at work. Every day of every year brings something new to learn about and appreciate. A mother can scarcely escape becoming somewhat of an authority on nutrition and vitamins, interior decorating, or sewing, or gardening. Her natural homemaking instincts have opportunities to become skilled tools.

If only we are not in too great a hurry, and are willing to take even a hen's pace to enjoy the opportunity to mature and grow through the ordinary family frame, we can be wife, mother, poet, musician, or whatever our gift may be. Techniques can be kept alive even through the busy years—letters and diaries for writing skills, piano playing for the children, appreciation of line and color in every sunset and tree, mental agility in answering the factual questions of the very young and evaluating questions of the adolescents.

Or we can develop an avocation. I was trained to be a teacher. I wanted to work at Hull House and to write. Not great novels, but articles for magazines. Then I married at twenty and put aside my ambitions. I sold my typewriter for fifteen dollars during our first struggling year. Husband, house, and children were to absorb my time. But they did not. I read at least five books a week those first seven years. Reading novels and going to plays help us to know ourselves. They provide a fine emotional outlet, but they give very little creative satisfaction. It was a Sunday school class that widened my horizon beyond homemaking.

A speaker at a mother's club told us that if we did not approve the way the Sunday schools were being run we should enroll as teachers. And I did! At odd moments throughout the week I was gathering materials, planning lessons, reading widely but for a purpose. Later on I began to write about our creative curriculum and to review books for religious periodicals. Teaching Sunday school was not a duty, not a bore, but an exciting adventure.

The serious artist, however, will not be willing to proceed at this slow pace. She will impose upon herself a rigorous discipline in order to create; at the same time she will bend every effort not to neglect her vocation of marriage. Harriette Arnow, an already established author, published practically nothing the first ten years of her married life. She says, "I had to develop a pattern of early rising in order to do anything at all. I start writing when I awaken, usually around four A.M." Five years were required to complete *Hunter's Horn.* Harriette Arnow is best known for *The Dollmaker,* one of the great novels of our generation. At the same deliberate pace she wrote the recently published *Seedtime Along the Cumberland,* a nonfiction study of pioneer days. The books within her had to find expression but never at the expense of her family.

Rebecca Caudill (Mrs. James S. Ayars) has written eleven fine children's books, among them *Tree of Freedom, The House of the Fifers, Susan Cornish* for teenagers; and *Happy Little Family, Schoolhouse in the Woods, Higgins and the Great Big Scare* for the 5 to 9 age group. When I met her we talked of a homemaker's difficulty in finding time to write. Her wise words implied that juvenile books are apt to be most wholesome if family and home come first in the author's life, and if the author participates to some extent in community and civic duties.

Mrs. Ayars says that her husband, an editor and an author, has played a vital role in her career as author. He encouraged her to begin writing; he is understanding and "easy to live with" when she becomes engrossed in a manuscript; and he has always been her severest and most constructive critic.

Indirectly, the Ayars children helped perfect their moth-

er's storytelling skill. As they dried dishes she often related
to them stories based on childhood incidents. Many of these
stories found their way into her books.

Mrs. Ayars scheduled her time for writing around her
home and family responsibilities, taking care always that
these came first. When the children were small, she used
their naptime and playtime for writing. When they started
to school, she spent the hours when they were in the school-
room writing in the library where reference books were
handy, and doorbell and telephone did not distract.

A PATTERN FOR WHOLENESS

Because of a special talent Harriette Arnow and Rebecca
Caudill have disciplined their lives. (Someone has defined
discipline as organization of energies.) But what about the
ordinary housewife? How is she to balance the many demands upon her time and interest?

This book has been written over the years by an ordinary
housewife. It is written primarily for the woman who gladly
gave up her job as secretary, nurse, or teacher to become a
wife and mother. Deep down she remains contented and
would not change the vocation of marriage for any other.
That does not prevent her pondering many times whether
or not the seeming scatteredness of her life has purpose and
pattern.

If the purpose of existence is to be useful, to exercise
one's particular gift, to grow more loving, to increase in
awareness of beauty and goodness, to be ever more thankful for the miracle of life, many selves seem to be required
for such fulfillment.

There may be one self who wants to bake golden loaves
of bread, wash the kitchen shelves, weed the garden, use
all the tangible domestic arts to create an orderly, well-
provisioned home. A second self desires to lie abed in the

morning, curl up all afternoon with a good novel, listen to good music, write stories, drink coffee, and laugh over the *New Yorker*. The third self is quite unhappy without the companionship of family and friends, without an outreach to those in trouble, or even a prominent part in the world of affairs. A fourth longs for solitude and an early rising that gives space in the day for prayer.

How can we pull together this divided creature? The bustling housewife! Sister Body motivated by the Brain of Pooh, caring for nothing but honey and condensed milk! The extrovert yearning for friends, social work, and a family of her own! The ascetic who longs for a solitary state of Nirvana! Instead of worrying about her diverse interests, she can learn to give thanks for the richness of her existence, for the wholeness she may attain as she weaves together the varying selves of her feminine nature.

A pattern should emerge in the weaving. Within the larger pattern of a whole life is the intricate design of the day. As the body is no less of God's making than the spirit, a precious wisdom has been gained when the rhythm in which body and soul best function is found. Fenelon stressed over and over, "Guard your mornings." At least the early hours may be planned once the children are in school. The early part of the day seems the best time for most of us to come close to the heart of God—to pray, to write, or to create whatever takes mind and soul. After that inward time, the body is still untired and can do outward things—household tasks, gardening, committees, friendly visiting, volunteer jobs. Evenings can be given to companionship—conversation, games, movies, music, reading, whatever recreation keeps us cheerful and free.

Out of the welter of pace and pattern the design that emerges is the old, old symbol, a cross. I see a cross as the signpost that directs us again and again as we wander too far afield or stay too long in some pleasant haven along the highway. I see the cross pointing us toward wholeness of life, directing us simultaneously to family and work, to recreation and prayer. The level of life on which women spend most of their time serving their families, friends, and community—that is the horizontal bar of the cross which seems to point in opposite directions but turns out to be all of a piece, with no separation between family and work.

Likewise the upright bar is unbroken. It can scarcely be determined where recreation which keeps life sane and joyful ceases, and spiritual renewal begins. Housework, the rearing of children, and the recreation which keeps those areas in balance may prove to be a triune base on which the spiritual life is founded. A woman at last discovers that love is the golden thread running throughout the pattern, binding all her seemingly disparate activities together. If she willingly accepts the slow pace and the seeming scatteredness of her years, her life will be blessed and give blessing.

2. God Setteth the Solitary in Families

CHANGE IS the one thing we can depend on. If instead of resisting change we can feel a rhythm to the years, feel that we are taking a useful and graceful part in the divine pattern of creation, life takes on purpose and meaning. A woman's life, from childhood and adolescence, young womanhood and early marriage, to middle and declining years can be a glorious evolution.

All of growth falls into stages. The unwanted tomato hornworm develops from egg to larva, to pupa, to night-flying moth with wings so swift in motion that its hovering flight resembles that of the welcome humming bird. If this is the natural process for the lowly caterpillar, how much more true it should be that all of human existence is meant to be a continuing cycle of growth. We are always in process of becoming that which we now are not. Character is in constant formation through continuing choices and ever fresh actions. It is never "a thing and a fact," von Huegel says, but "an act and an energy." We make a mistake to pigeonhole ourselves or our children. No one should be placed in a fixed category as if he could not change.

Although the moth or butterfly breaks through its chrysalis with automatic timing, human beings must will to shed the tight skin of their self-love. Sun and warmth are neces-

10

sary to change the pupa to the winged creature; God's grace is necessary to us, and is as freely given as the sunshine. But we must will to cooperate with his grace, to recognize and lay hold of the powers that everywhere reach out to guide and bless our progress. That "God setteth the solitary in families" is one measure of his grace. We are blessed not only by being members of a particular family, but also by belonging to the family of man.

That proud, indifferent, cynical, separate self begins to change when belief grows that love is the greatest thing in the world. Once we accept the premise that the purpose of life is to love God and serve him, to become his friends, finally to become the sons of God, for whom the creation waits with eager longing; then we can also believe that God hath set us in families for the most perfect accomplishment of that plan.

WE CHOOSE TO MARRY

A family begins with the union of man and woman. And a married couple is a family, whether or not children are born to them. Even if they become parents, the two of them remain a family unit when the children are grown. This chapter, therefore, is mainly concerned with the relationship between husband and wife. In our country and in our day, we do not have marriage thrust upon us. We have done what we wanted to do. Now how are we best to appreciate this good thing that we have got?

In *The Recovery of Family Life* Pauline Trueblood says that past generations of women made enduring marriages because of an old wives' wisdom that was handed down from mother to daughter. If that knowledge is now a lost art, some of us old wives who are happily married had better share our secrets. Perhaps we have something to say that is not found in the learned books written by doctors, psychiatrists, and marital counselors.

Not that I mean to belittle books as guides, for I draw constantly upon them for direction and inspiration. Rather than scientific and theoretical studies, however, the books that light my path are likely to be poems, biographies, and novels. I wish therefore to quote at length from the two books which reaffirmed my faltering hope that a winsome, joyful, and lasting wedded state could be achieved. I had heard my mother say too often that there was no such thing as a truly happy marriage. Perhaps it was James and Lucretia Mott's loving life together as well as their high principles and abiding faith that made me want to be a Quaker. Three weeks after their wedding in 1811, James and Lucretia Mott received from his mother a loving letter filled with sound advice:

> I will hazard the sentiment, that if it is your united endeavor to make each other happy, ten years hence, on comparing your feelings and measuring your affection by what you now consider its greatest height, you will gratefully acknowledge that the early days of wedded life are but the dawn of that happiness which is attached to it. Yet do not mistake me; I do not wish for you to look for an unclouded sky; this is not the lot of mortals; but only to believe that, by doing all in your power to *deserve* the blessing of sincere and unbroken love to each other, you will find that love so increased as to become an asylum of rest when all other temporal supports fail. . . . But beware, my beloved children, of supposing that even the most ardent affection can give that happiness which the maternal breast craves for you, should your hearts rest only in each other; raise them to Him, who has already blessed in joining you together, and who will continue to bless, if there is a disposition to estimate His favors rightly."[1]

---

[1] *Life and Letters of James and Lucretia Mott,* edited by Anna Davis Hallowell, pp. 43-44. Houghton Mifflin Company, 1884.

That this old-fashioned language with its eternal wisdom
had good effect on the young Motts is proved by a letter
James Mott wrote years later concerning the marriage of
their daughter:

> Yes, Martha is married, and we feel lonely. That many are dis-
> appointed in the marriage state, I have no doubt; but that "not
> one in a thousand but is doomed to disappointment," I do not
> believe. I have lived in that state for more than forty years,
> and it has been one of harmony and love, though we have
> had our trials and difficulties in life. As age advances, our
> love, if possible, increases. This being my experience, I am in
> favor of matrimony and wish to see all for whom I feel in-
> terested made happy in that way. It is the natural state of
> man, and when rightly entered into, an increase of happi-
> ness and comfort is the certain result.[2]

The second book from which I wish to quote is my favorite novel, *Come Spring*, which is based on the diaries kept
by ordinary people during the American Revolution. At his
wife's suggestion, Joel Adams had just decided to call the
men of the community together to sign another petition to
send to the General Court. (Women voted indirectly in
those days.)

> Mima said, "They'll get so they look to you to tell 'em what
> to do. . . . You're a good man, Joel. Men listen to you."
> He said laughingly: "You keep on telling me how smart
> I am and you'll have me believing it." Then he added more
> seriously: "I wasn't much, you know, till you got hold of me.
> But you're so sure I'm going to—work hard and do right—that
> I have to do it to keep you from being disappointed."
> "I guess that's the way with men," she agreed. "A woman's
> the root and a man's the tree. She's the ground he grows out
> of. That's a wife's job; to be good growing ground, so her man
> will be fine."

---

[2] *Ibid.,* p. 337.

"What if she isn't? Say she's sour land, or sandy, or dry?"

"Then he'll be a stunted sort of a man, or else he'll find another woman, that's all. A man don't go far without some woman loving him and always telling him he's wonderful."

He said, half to himself: "If I was a tree, I needed pruning pretty bad when you took hold of me, Mima." After a moment he added: "I still do, for the matter of that. I ain't all you keep telling me I am; but I mean to be. If you keep on telling me, I'll get to be." There was a deep tenderness in his tones. "You're good growing ground, Mima."[3]

So having chosen to be good growing ground, let us be thankful for this human love bestowed upon us, thankful that we have trees to hold our earth in place—to keep us from becoming barren, eroded, washed-away and wasted soil. God deliver us from being Mrs. Tullivers or Mrs. Jelly-bys. Remember how George Eliot's character had a gift for saying things that drove her husband in just the opposite direction to her desire; how Dickens' Mrs. Jellyby went off to Borrioboola-gha to save the poor heathen children from sin, leaving her own husband and young ones unloved and unnurtured.

EVERYONE NEEDS LOVE AND APPROVAL

Instead of being the ground out of which a new and enlarging relationship can grow, some of us marry, and then want to hold back. We are like Saint Augustine when he prayed, "Make me a Christian but not yet," or like the young mother in childbirth who agonized, "I've changed my mind. I've changed my mind." Too often in following the modern career pattern we cry, "Make me a helpmeet but not yet."

There are some sloughs of despond from which we should

[3] *Come Spring* by Ben Ames Williams, p. 729. Houghton Mifflin Company, 1940. Used by permission.

turn back; there may be some divorces that are right. But considering the unhappy children who crawl out of such wrecks, to say nothing of the men and women warped by such a faith-shattering experience, on the whole marriage is and should be almost as irrevocable as birth or death. Some married lives are naturally beautiful as are the blue-bells and spring beauties. But some must be cultivated, lifted like the tulips when they become too crowded, and reset, and enriched.

One divorce was about to occur because the husband felt his wife gave too much time to her music. She was hurt because he did not applaud her talent, and because he never took her out socially. Some marriages would be happier if the husbands could praise their wives, for whatever it is that a woman puts her heart into—her acting in plays; her cooking; her chairing of a committee. There is something in a woman that craves spoken recognition from her husband, no matter how much the world says, "Well done." One wife says that if her spouse had ever commended her labors, she would have worked herself to a frazzle trying to measure up. Another keeps trying to buy a French face cream, no longer manufactured, because once her husband said how sweet a fragrance she wore.

Now I am sure there are ways we fail our men that we need to learn about. The female lioness tends to rear her independent head when the honeymoon is over, and we forget that a woman's peculiar contribution is to be the interpreter, the relater, the comforter of her little kingdom. It is Christ the Lamb within her that needs to emerge. As the sexual urge decreases with advancing years it is of paramount importance that tenderness increase. Grown-ups are children at heart and they need always a show of affection.

In one home, I remember watching the wife rise as her husband opened the front door, returning after his long day at work; I remember the shine in this middle-aged woman's eyes, the love in her voice as she said, "Here comes the best husband in all the world."

In another house, each evening the husband returned halfheartedly; he never knew how he would be greeted—perhaps with silence, occasionally pleasantly, sometimes with a strident demanding tone, "Edgar, don't tell me you're here at last."

The men are sometimes asked, "Are you a mouse or a man?" We women might ask ourselves, "Am I a lion or a lamb?" Is the caring, loving side taking command rather than the critical, analytical intellect? If my husband were a poet, could he give thanks for order and peace and beauty, could he pay tribute to the artist in his home, as does Archibald MacLeish?

> This poem is for my wife
> I have made it plainly and honestly
> The mark is on it
> Like the burl on the knife
>
> I have not made it for praise
> She has no more need for praise
> Than the summer has
> Or the bright days
>
> In all that becomes a woman
> Her words and her ways are beautiful
> Love's lovely duty
> The well-swept room
>
> Wherever she is there is sun
> And time and a sweet air
> Peace is there
> Work done

There are always curtains and flowers
And candles and baked bread
And a cloth spread
And a clean house

Her voice when she sings is a voice
At dawn by a freshening sea
Where the wave leaps in the
Wind and rejoices

Wherever she is it is now
It is here where the apples are
Here in the stars
In the quick hour

The greatest and richest good—
My own life to live in—
This she has given me
If giver could[4]

But suppose the idealized companionship coveted by young couples does not develop. Probably most middle-aged people, if honest, would have to acknowledge that there have been moments when the idea of a separation at least crossed their minds. Must their marriage vows—"For better or worse, for richer or poorer"—become a lie; their hope of being "heirs of life and grace together" be damned?

For those who choose divorce as the way out, new difficulties arise. In one big city church the minister and his wife had the imagination to see the needs of divorced women and to invite them to meet each other. These women have been thankful to find how similar are their problems, to talk over their loneliness under the wise leadership of a reli-

[4] "Poem in Prose" in *Actfive and Other Poems* by Archibald MacLeish, pp. 48-49. Random House, 1948. Used by permission.

giously motivated psychiatrist. Most of them admit that if they could live their lives over, they would not choose divorce. However grievous the difficulties of living together, the difficulties of living alone are greater.

Often affection ripens late between those who in their early wedded life bickered over money, infidelity, liquor, means of livelihood, or lack of social activity. One old lady remarked, "Aye, we had our quarrels in the early days, but the last six years we had together made up for all of that."

A HOUSE UPON A ROCK

Mark Twain once observed that no couple could begin to know the bliss of being married, short of twenty-five years together. In the presence of a companionable middle-aged pair, young romance seems a feeble reed in comparison to the strong plant of their devotion. How have they weathered the storms and reached such a mature affection, that their shining joy in being together is a blessing to all who touch their lives?

Helpful techniques can always be discovered from experiences of families who have pulled through the years together. For the solid rock upon which the good family remains firm is a pudding stone composed of adaptability, companionship, and a determination to stick together. Let us consider some of the well-worn pebbles that comprise the conglomerate rock upon which a staunch and faithful family builds.

Adaptability

One mother changed her entire outlook on life by making a chart for herself. She said that she had become so slipshod around the house that she was thoroughly tired of herself. She listed several items that would make life pleasanter for each member of the family. For her husband she would get up in time to have an unhurried breakfast, have the house neat when he returned from work, and a good supper ready. For her children she would avoid those areas where they disliked being pushed around. She was to start them off cheerfully to school, and to bed; be patient while helping them with music and reading. For herself she was to stop eating sweet things and do her exercises. Any day she made a perfect score, she allowed herself a piece of Camembert cheese before going to bed! It was such a struggle for self-discipline that she sometimes felt like a nun retiring from the world. Some day we may have the biography telling of the growth and unfolding of all the six members of that family.

In our house, one of the saving techniques is known as the "Papa Please List." Anything I want done—spading a flower bed, moving a trunk, putting on the screens, going with me to call on the new neighbors—gets written on a scrap of paper and hung upon a certain nail. Having written down these masculine chores, I am never allowed to mention them. Of course, if the spring is getting far advanced and seeds are not yet planted, I may remark, "Have you looked at the Papa Please List lately?" Only those who try this procedure can appreciate the amount of nagging that disappears. A husband who saw our list asked, "Why not a Mama Please List?" When he returned home and introduced such a device, his wife said she learned for the first time of her husband's annoyance at never finding clean bathroom towels on laundry day.

A country minister and his wife tried trading jobs for a week. Just to imagine such an experience brings a feeling of tolerance. Did father have to curl the little girl's hair and mend the family wash? How did mother make out driving a load of grain to the elevator and preparing the weekly sermon? Criticism diminishes and flexibility increases when we put ourselves in the other's place.

"My husband doesn't talk to me" is the complaint of many wives. We might ask ourselves, "Are we ready to listen at the time they want to talk?" One husband may spill over the minute he walks into the kitchen. His wife, washing a child's face with one hand and stirring the gravy with the other, wishes his conversation could at least wait until they sit down at the supper table. Another man tends to be silent all evening but awakens his wife at four-thirty to thresh out with him a new invention or the predicament in the Middle East!

A friend of mine moaned over her husband's inability to communicate until she made an extended visit in a talkative household. There, every minute decision, every small anxiety, each trivial incident was worried aloud: "What tie shall I wear?" "Are you sure this fish is fresh?" "The neighbors are using our dropped apples!" No comfortable, compatible, unexpressed trust in life seemed to exist. Home once more, my friend never again felt critical of her reticent husband. Instead, each day she rejoices in a love that undergirds and underlies their relationship even though unspoken. Let us learn to be sensitive listeners when our men want to talk. And if they don't, can't we let them be themselves and love them as they are?

The use of their money is a frequent sore point between husbands and wives, as was illustrated by a recent George Clark cartoon: "My husband and I like the same thing—but I like to spend it and he likes to save it." Sometimes a man drives himself so hard to get ahead in business, works such long hours, that there is no leisure to give to his wife, no good-natured companionship to spend on his children. Of course it may be the wife's inordinate desire for finery, for keeping up with the neighbors that drives a man to holding down two jobs. Sometimes one of them feels that an ever mounting hoard of stocks and bonds is the only security. Long, long ago it was realized that the love of money can be the root of much evil.

So much publicity is given to women's buying power, so much advertising is directed toward them as potential spenders, that it is hard to believe women still exist who must ask their husbands for every cent they spend. Victorian though it may sound, such thwarted ones do live in these United States here and now: women who suffer because their husbands will not spend a cent on recreation, will give them no personal allowance, will see them and the children shabbily dressed rather than put one less dollar in their ever-increasing saving funds.

If only tenderness and consideration for each other could grow between them, the husband would want to make some gifts to his wife as a material expression of his love. She, in turn, would recognize her own tendencies toward frivolous spending, and would be glad of his protective thoughtfulness of her old age. She would give thanks for her mate's many fine qualities, which she has a tendency to take for granted. A heart to heart talk and the exercise of reason on the part of both might save them from the necessity of seeking help from a marriage clinic, or worse, resorting to divorce.

A husband needs to understand a woman's feminine hunger to have some money for which she need not account, as well as a budgeted amount for clothing. After all, she wants to dress well not only to make herself attractive to him, but also to keep her own self-respect. Likewise she needs to remember how in their courtship days and as a bride it was always her desire to please her husband. Desire and delight and love are better motives than duty. But whatever the motive, no marriage can last unless each partner is willing to give in to the other on some matters. Principles and ideals

are seldom threatened, but in day-to-day details why should
the wives always insist on being humored? So much of modern literature, including cartoons, suggests that women want
to have their own way, willy-nilly.

Fenelon's advice to a seventeenth century lady is pertinent today. "As to dress, it seems to me you ought to consider Monsieur de Montberon's tastes and wishes. If he
thinks economy necessary, you should retrench as much as
possible; if he wishes you to keep up a certain external style,
do whatever he seems to desire, simply to please him, not
to indulge your own tastes. If he leaves you to your own
judgment in this matter, I should say that medium was the
best self-denial for you. You are inclined to extremes; your
pride and fastidiousness would stop short of nothing but
perfect magnificence; and severe simplicity is but another
refinement of self-will; it is a splendid renunciation of splen-
dor. But the mid-course is the trying one."[5]

As comfortable means increase, couples are apt to lean
toward penuriousness or extravagance unless they deliberately plan a middle course. Newlyweds, however, usually
have litle choice as to whether or not they will struggle to
economize. And their parents probably suffer more over the
problems that lie ahead of them than do the bride and groom
themselves. So writes one mother: "I have such mixed feel-
ings about Jim and Hazel and their starting out. I know
how many disappointments there are; how many injustices;
how much strength is called for. In short, I know it is a
struggle. Then I bring myself up short and remember that
without struggle there is no gain, and that opposition makes
one stronger. I remember the financial end, with not enough
to do what one would like to do, but then I recall that we

---

[5] *Letters to Women* by Francois Fenelon. E. P. Dutton and Company, 1893.

had our most wonderful times as a family on our lowest salaries."

Companionship

In marriage counseling classes great stress is laid upon the need for engaged young couples to have many things in common. Certainly it is fine if they both like to play bridge, both like to go to baseball games, but married life can also be rich and satisfying if each mate brings different skills and interests to the partnership. Discussing community of interests my husband laughed and said, "There just wouldn't be time enough for you to listen to all the baseball games with me, and for me to go to all your poetry clubs with you." Probably the crux of the matter is whether or not a man and wife find mutual friends and companionable interests as they both mature.

One woman liked the theater, and her husband enjoyed musical comedies. She liked to read; he said he had had enough books in college to last the rest of his life. She liked to play bridge; he relaxed while fishing. Now they live far away from a metropolitan district, and there are few tickets to buy to anything. There is little time for either to read, because they both love gardening, both enjoy poking about in antique shops, both are enthusiastic ornithologists. In time companionship grows, or at least tolerance and respect for difference develops. A husband's pleasure in fishing and fishing tackle is no longer "trash" to his wife! And he comes to understand her need for feminine society, whether it be for playing bridge or reading poetry.

It is much easier to stay happily married when moving in a society comprised of well-wedded couples. Indeed a man and woman should withdraw from a social group where ridiculing, belittling, and bitter joking prevail, just as surely as they would turn back from the edge of a precipice. It takes a very strong bird to flit among birds who are pulling out each other's feathers without losing a few plumes, or worse, a mate. When two young lovers promise to be faithful to each other "until death do us part," fidelity in words is a part of that vow.

If their conversation in public is to be spontaneously respectful of each other—and not just a biting of the tongue—their words must flow from an inward trust and assurance of love. While surface interests need not be mutual, partners in a strong marriage are likely to have in common the deep things of life.

The Roman Catholic Church is sound in its practice of encouraging couples to gather in the company of a teaching priest for a retreat. One year in the San Bernardino foothills fifty-five couples spent three days in recreation and worship together. For eighteen years the Holy Family Retreat Association has been helping husbands and wives to love each other more deeply, as their human love becomes more firmly rooted and grounded in the love of God. Many of the churches are now holding family institutes from which the parents return with a new perspective and fresh dedication.

One marriage counselor said that her class was shocked when she expressed the belief that there are harder things to endure than infidelity. Often a lack of physical faithfulness is tied in with a person's lack of faith in himself, or lack of faith in God. Or just plain loneliness may be the cause.

Mima, in *Come Spring*, knew that no matter how momentarily Joel was attracted to the other woman his love for her was staunch and true, and that eventually they could begin and build on an immovable foundation. Such intuitive discernment did not prevent Mima from suffering. It did give her an inner sureness, a serenity with which to rebuild their shaken union. Let it be said that Joel did resist Mily's advances. Let it also be said that more men and women flee from such temptations than is commonly supposed. While the Kinsey report gave statistics proving that man is a polygamous creature, the other side of that report is rarely stressed. Consider the miracle of 50 per cent of all married couples continuing steadfast and loyal to each other. Jesus gave us a high conception of marriage: "God, from the first days of creation made them man and woman. A man, therefore, will leave his father and mother and will cling to his wife." That so great a number hold to high ideals of constancy and devotion is cause for thanksgiving. If there has been failure to achieve an idyllic union, what spiritual values, what reservoir of strength can be drawn upon to bind a family together during the times of difficulty?

Determination

Differences of taste and temperament need not destroy the bond of marriage if there is a determination to succeed. If a community of interests does not develop between husband and wife a workable marriage can still be achieved. Individuals with a sense of dignity, with a feeling of responsibility, can make an asset and strength of their differences in order to create a good home for their children. I know this from personal experience.

My mother was very devout, spending what little time she could reading literature of inspiration. My father read novels. My mother loved classical music and church hymns. My father liked gay popular music and folk songs. My mother's week turned around her attendance at church. My father seldom went to any religious service. My mother did not care about picnics, though I must say she packed the lunch basket full of fried chicken and homemade bread and sometimes went along on our country outings. My father loved the woods and fields, knew every tree and flower and bird in Illinois. My mother thought that whatever was worth doing was worth doing well. My father would mend a broken fence with whatever piece of old lumber or baling wire was at hand. My mother was reserved. My father was affable and outgoing, enjoying card games and croquet.

This is enough to indicate that they might have dissolved their marriage on the grounds of incompatibility. But they stayed together and gave their five children affection and security. We went to our mother with our troubles. We went with our father to the movies and on wonderful expeditions in the spring to see the new-born lambs and tiny "calico" pigs, in the fall to gather hickory nuts and persimmons. Each parent made an important contribution to the life of the family. We learned early that there is not just one kind of behavior essential to a good life, nor one philosophy compatible with the search for truth.

And as a difference in temperament and taste is not sufficient ground for separation, neither is immaturity. Certainly some young people are better balanced emotionally than others. The road of marriage has enough hills and valleys without knowingly choosing an unstable partner for the journey. From every Dorothy Dix column flow warnings that marriage should never be undertaken with the purpose of reform in mind. Nevertheless, intentionally or not, people cannot help changing each other.

One who changed me, I came to call "Mother Currier." For twenty years we wrote to each other. She shared with me her love of poetry, good books, hard work, beauty, humor, religious faith. Throughout these chapters, I would share with you some of her insights. When her husband became ill in body and mind, even turning against her, Mother Currier learned to pause each time when entering the sick room and to pray inwardly, "God bless you, Ralph." It not only made that difficult condition bearable, she said, but such an inward salutation would work wonders upon any grumpy, disagreeable person.

Some couples who seem to have very little religious faith achieve an enduring and satisfying union. But it must be difficult to build on human strength alone. Any relationship is the finer for having been held up in prayer to the Source of all love. It is impossible not to love a person for whom one prays.

The Mizpah benediction—"May the Lord watch between thee and me while we are absent one from the other"—need not be reserved just for the times when a couple are separated from each other. It is not being alone, however, that makes a person lonely, but feeling forgotten. He who knows that he is being carried in the heart of the beloved can endure long separations. But when the members of a household press too closely upon each other, it is imperative to ask the good Lord to "watch between thee and me" while we are together!

In a rightly founded marriage, the unity of man and wife can be symbolic of the unity they seek to find with God. A woman's prayer might be: "As I give myself in love and joy to my husband and learn to be aware of his presence and needs, help me, O God, to be just as aware of thy presence and of thy will and purpose for me."

Maturity is attained as the core of love at the center spreads into ever increasing areas of application. For indifference and self-centeredness are sloughed away as a person grows in the sense of being one with another and another and another. The individual is born into the isolated nest of his individual family. Life began for him with a particular family unit. But life's purpose for him is achieved only when the individual feels himself related to God and all his creation. From the adventure of life in one human family we move on to membership in the family of God, where not a single one of his children is beyond our caring. God hath set us in families for the perfect accomplishment of his plan, a plan in which we begin to learn that love is the greatest thing in the world.

3. The High Emprize of Motherhood

I come in the little things,
Saith the Lord:
Yea! on the glancing wings
Of eager birds, the softly pattering feet
Of furred and gentle beasts, I come to meet
Your hard and wayward heart. In brown bright eyes
That peep from out the brake, I stand confest.
On every nest
Where feathery Patience is content to brood
And leaves her pleasure for the high emprize
Of motherhood—
There doth my Godhead rest.[1]

SEXUAL LOVE between husband and wife is good and beautiful, and for most people, the beginning of learning to care for someone else more than themselves. When the children come along the ego gets whittled down a little more. Our hearts begin to be made tender by the existence of these small helpless infants, entirely dependent upon the self-centered immature parents that most of us are in the early years of marriage. Experts say that the parents increase in maturity with the birth of each child.

---

[1] "Immanence" in *Immanence: A Book of Verses* by Evelyn Underhill, p. 1. E. P. Dutton and Company, 1912. Used by permission.

I want to pay tribute to the young parents of today. They are doing a better job than we did in my generation, perhaps than has ever been done. Certainly they bring more intelligence and just as much caring to the problems that confront them. Groups of young parents with whom I have met—Episcopalians, Quakers, Methodists, Presbyterians, Congregationalists—are sincere and eager to make an art of parenthood.

METHODS AND MISTAKES

Thirty years ago we were so intent on following the right method, that some of us did more harm than good by bringing up our children in a strained and tense and too prescribed atmosphere. We were over-earnest. We played bridge by Holt instead of Hoyle. We had too many books. It was about us that Tim in *Rabbit Hill* spoke at least a half-truth: "Reading rots the mind." Of course there have always been some wise mothers who held to a golden mean through all fads and extremes, like the mother of the four famous Comptons who summed up their formula of success briefly: "We used the Bible and common sense." How fortunate it is that the present-day pediatric authority, Dr. Spock, recommends common sense.

We need not be anxious about methods and techniques. We need to love our children, to accept them as individuals and to enjoy them. Of course, we will make mistakes. But we are not the final word in shaping them, any more than our parents were in molding us. The chief way we influence our children is by being the best we know how to be ourselves. That will be more lasting than whether or not we spank them. Any method of discipline can be good if it is rooted in love. Speaking of a nursery school child who was a bit of a problem, the teacher once commented, "I do not love him enough to spank him."

That mother wit has regained its rightful place is shown in the following letter: "We need constantly to discipline ourselves to be flexible, physically, so we can clean under the beds occasionally, or hide things on closet shelves—and in our habits so that we can get up at three in the morning to set the table if necessary. And emotionally because so often the woman of the household has to be the clearing ground for the various individualities in the family. If her emotional reactions dominate, the conflicts will be more acute. We must be flexible spiritually because our role will change with the years, as our children grow and leave home and become parents themselves; we must be prepared to grow with them and to accept the tide of change, while keeping in touch with the changeless too."

My grandmother knew how to keep in touch with the changeless. I remember well hearing her counsel asked by a young mother who was troubled about the conduct of her son. The young woman exclaimed, "Goodness knows, I have told him often enough what he ought to do." And Grandmother replied, "Actions speak louder than words. And don't forget to pray and sing." To have been brought up in an atmosphere of song is to have been left an inheritance that is a lasting legacy.

Singing hymns as one works seems a simple method of vocal prayer. Hymns and poems can be memorized while ironing or mending instead of looking at television. Early settlers memorized the Bible as they spun and wove, not in tenseness or anxiety but in quiet reverence. This method of praise and prayer, of keeping in touch with the changeless, does not need the voice of a Marian Anderson or even a facile memory. The power to remember will come if one really cares.

Yet those of us who have missed opportunities and made grievous mistakes can take heart from the wise counsel written by Father Tyrell to no less a saint than Baron von Huegel. "I was sorry to gather from your letter that you were fretting about Gertrude; and by fretting I mean chafing over mistakes made in the past in all good faith, such as the wisest and best of us must often make; which no amount of fretting will remedy, but only trust in God who turns our blunders to greater eventual gain than our skill would ever effect."[2]

With von Huegel, we too must learn not to fret over mistakes. We can do the best we know how, we can be honest about our beliefs, and yet the children may learn the most from what we dislike, or turn against what we are intensely enthusiastic about. One mother who was an ardent botanist and bird lover exposed her sons directly and repeatedly to her hobbies, yet neither son ever had any real passion for rare flower or bird's flight. The final reaction and escape of one of them was to flunk the zoology course in college, the only low mark he ever received!

No, we cannot predict. Having children is much more of an exciting adventure than it would be if we had certainty that they would model after us. The hope is that they will go far beyond us and perhaps in some quite undreamed of field of work and vision. They may at least look upon mundane tasks in a different spirit. A Quaker educator says she loves work, especially washing dishes, because the women of her home hated the chore. A little girl told me, "When I grow up I'm going to be an angel; my sister is going to be a housewife, or maybe a housekeeper." May we pray not to hinder them from being true originals, whether it leads to homemaking, or the bearing of good tidings.

Some young parents may fear they have failed to give their children security because of frequent changes of resi-

---

[2] *Selected Letters* by Baron Frederick von Huegel. J. M. Dent and Company.

dence. One of our children's teachers comforted me over
an uprooting, when she said, "Do not worry about moving
your children. They will become more adaptable and less
conservative in adult life because of these childhood adjust-
ments." Being the son of a minister, my husband lived in
many houses from Vermont to California. The children and
their father are as "secure" as I who spent my first twenty
years in the same house.

Without doubt a few household treasures moved from
house to house can help make a home. You may remember
how delighted George Eliot's Maggie was to see her old copy
of *Pilgrim's Progress* when the *Mill on the Floss* possessions
seemed to have been swept away forever. But the real home
is first of all dependent on something more tangible than
ancient samplers and grandma's teapot.

It is the love that counts, the relationship of father and
mother to each other and to the children. During the bomb-
ing of Okinawa the breast-fed babies strapped to their
mothers' backs suffered amazingly little from fright. Their
security came from proximity to the protecting person
rather than a geographical spot called home.

WHERE PATIENCE BROODS

Feathery patience leaves her pleasure, but she gains treasure—yes, a thousandfold. The patience of the bird on a nest
is only the beginning of a mother's patience. For the first
and most required element of a parent's love is patience.
But it must be a real deep-seated patience. As you well
know, we can never fool our children with any outward
show of virtue that does not stem from the heart.

One little boy had called his mother back a half dozen
times for another drink or another confidence, or to remind
her she had forgotten to repeat, "The dark is kind and cozy."
She was getting a little worn. Then he said, "Why are you

mad, Mother?" She had been so sure that she was behaving in a calm and patient manner. "Why, what makes you think I am cross?" "You walk mad."

No, we cannot deceive them. A little girl labeled her painting "People who have lost their train." Her sister asked, "Why are they so furious? Won't there be another train?" The small artist answered, "Of course, in a minute, but when I paint grown-up faces, I always make them furious. That shows right away that they are grown-up."[3]

Oh, do they never see us anything but furious, or hear us walk any way but mad?

Patience can never come without awareness and understanding. Many mothers have a wisdom of the heart, a fund of homely truth, a quality of divine ordinariness that often goes unnoticed in this career-centered, materialistic country of ours. Bronson Alcott had first-hand experience of this quality. "Was not his mother a far wiser, kinder, gentler, and in every way better person than the schoolmistress? And what could that mean, unless that there are more important things in the world than reading, writing, and exact knowledge of the length of the Zambesi River. His mother knew things too, although one never found them set down in books, and even she seldom tried to say them in words. She said them in the way she acted, in the touch of her hand, in the smile of her eyes."[4]

Some women, like Bronson Alcott's mother, are naturally good mothers. Some must learn the art of parenthood and they can. Again it was a book that helped me, made me terribly conscious of my busyness, my blindness. At the bare thought of the possibility of losing one of my children I

[3] *My Darling from the Lions* by Edita Morris, p. 12. The Viking Press, 1943. Used by permission.

[4] *Pedlar's Progress:* The Life of Bronson Alcott by Odell Shepard, p. 14. Little, Brown and Company, 1938. Used by permission of Odell Shepard.

determined to stop and look, really to see, really to listen, not only to their words, but to unspoken communications.

Do you remember that poignant passage in *Our Town?* If not, do get the play and read it again. You may weep, but the tears will clear the blindness from your eyes. Emily Gibbs has just died giving birth to her second child. She asks and is permitted to return to earth to live over again her twelfth birthday. Her mother, busy about breakfast, does not notice her. Emily, hurt by this casual attitude, cries out passionately, "Oh, Mama, just look at me one minute as though you really saw me. . . . Just for a moment now we're all together—Mama, just for a moment let's be happy. Let's look at one another!" Then Emily begins to sob, "I can't go on! It goes so fast. We don't have time to look at one another. . . . Take me back—up the hill—to my grave. But first: Wait! One more look! Goodby, Goodby, world! Goodby, Grover's Corners . . . Mama and Papa. Goodby to clocks ticking . . . and Mama's sunflowers. And food and coffee. And new-ironed dresses and hot baths . . . and sleeping and waking up. Oh, earth, you're too wonderful for anyone to realize you. Do any human beings ever realize life while they live it—every, every minute?"[5]

The answer in the play was, "Saints and poets maybe—they do *some.*" The following experience shows how a mother can learn to be aware, *some* of the time. It had been a full and happy weekend with many interesting things to do, and there were still activities that Peter wanted time to carry out before his return to school Monday morning. But the homework had been put off long enough, and his mother said that now he must settle down and finish before he started another thing. She sat down in the same room, apparently to read,

---

[5] *Our Town* by Thornton Wilder, pp. 123-125. Coward-McCann, 1938. Used by permission of Harper and Brothers.

but really to see that Peter did not waste any more time. Peter sat there too, sprawled out in the easiest chair, simply leafing through his English and science, his mind far away and intent on what he really wanted to do next. And his mother sat there not seeing the words, or at least not absorbing the meaning of her book, and feeling herself getting tighter and tighter, and tenser and tenser, until all she wanted to do was to scream, and what she did do was to scold in nagging voice: "Peter, you can't learn a thing that way. Are you really prepared in your English? Can I help you?" And so on.

Well, maybe she did not nag; most of us would have, we would not have been able to keep even a glowering silence. (Though what usually makes us want to scream is the exaggeration of our own faults we see in our children.)

And then into her overtaut mind and body almost filled with hate came an insight of love. The mother looked at Peter with fresh appreciation as if she had never seen him before, or might never see him again. She reached for a pencil and paper, and began to write, no longer observant whether or not Peter was settling down to study. And she wrote and wrote. "My son, my son. This is the child conceived in love that I myself bore. He is more precious to me than life itself." And she listed his sweet, lovable, helpful, and endearing qualities.

Having made this evaluation in a state of relaxed awareness, the mother looked up to find her son had moved to a straight chair and a table. He was upright and intensely poring over his books. Soon he got up and went out into the garden and came back with flowers in his hand calling, "Mother, come and look. Come and see. Here is the stamen and the pistil just as it shows in our book and, Mother, isn't it wonderful the way flowers are made so neatly?"

Surely we human beings can realize life at least some of

the minutes. The children learn from us—fury about missing the train, or the source of relaxed awareness and appreciation. We hardened old adults can learn from them, if we will but listen. They are filled with wonder, reverence, curiosity. They are without prejudice. They demand fairness. They want their parents to behave seemly. I am always thankful when I've been catty, sharp-tongued, ungenerous, to be brought to my senses by one of my children saying, "Don't talk like that, Mother!" Quakers speak of "eldering" when they are corrected by another or given counsel. When our children keep us growing, we call it being "youngered."

From our children we learn, if we have not before, the necessity to respect the treasures, the hobbies, the concerns, the contributions of each individual. From a piece of broken glass our daughter's interest in minerals may have developed. She and her dad were walking in the woods, scuffling through the leaves having a companionable time. Suddenly the little girl reached down and picked up a fragment of a blue milk of magnesia bottle. "I wouldn't pick that up," her father said, "it's just a piece of trash." She youngered him by retorting, "Daddy, it may be trash to you, but it is not trash to me!"

I am not very clear on my theological beliefs. I suppose children are born with a measure of original sin, but mainly I believe they come "trailing clouds of glory." If we listen we catch a bit of this glory—fresh, unspoiled points of view, unprejudiced observations, unconventional phrases. Read Hughes Mearn's *Creative Power* and *Creative Youth,* if you are missing this experience with your children. And sit up, or kneel down, and praise the Lord, each time one of them catches you tense and reminds you, "Take it easy, Toots." "It's all right, Mum, smile. Don't panic." "Never mind spilling the blackberries, Mother, more berries will grow there now, and we had fun picking them." "We'll make the train, don't run, Mum. The thing to do is to watch the clock instead of the people." And rejoice when they can tell with glee about the time you spanked them with the heel of your bedroom slipper, and the whole thing was unfair. If it is told, it won't fester down in the deeps. We pray, "Love is patient and kind; . . . it is not irritable," and hope this conscious desire and prayer will be changed by the grace of God to love that is spontaneously patient and understanding. But the children, they love us and cherish us through all our myriad mistakes.

They forgive us. God forgives us. We must also forgive ourselves. At times the children are bound to be naughty and exasperating; at times we are bound to be tired and cross. While learning to be patient with them, we must be patient with ourselves.

RELIGION AND READING ALOUD

I remember well a talk given at a mothers' meeting on the importance of religious attitudes, of listening to children and answering their questions seriously. In the question period a mother asked, "But when is there time for this— between dancing school, music, Scouts, late dinners, homework, and the parents' need of social life?" What do any of us really possess except our time and our wills? Should we not put our schedules into shape so that we do have time for a quiet period with each child each evening?

The questions will not be easy to answer. "Where was I before I was born?" "What is the really, really me?" "Do animals have souls?" "Is there a devil?" "Is it ever right to tell a lie?" "Do good people ever go to prison?" Many a parent has had to think through his own religious beliefs, to develop a philosophy of life, in order to answer his children.

Often young parents are puzzled as to whether or not they should teach their children prayers. If it is a choice between mechanical family prayers, or an atmosphere where the children sense their parents' dependence upon prayer, and observe the gentler, more loving people such practice produces, I should be content to let the children escape a set ritual. But since we do share with our children other things we love and find meaningful—good food, great music, the best books, delight in the stars, the wonder of migrating birds, the way the earth evolved—how can we help sharing what we honestly feel about our heavenly Father, about Jesus, and about the Christ Spirit?

But we must be honest. When the parent does not know, through lack of knowledge or of faith, she must say, "I do not know." If she does not pray, or believe in the power of prayer, mother had better skip the prayers and read aloud from a good book.

"This is the best part of the day," my daughter used to say of our reading and talking together after her young brother was asleep. Jealousy disappears as stories of happy families are shared between mother and older child. Years ago *Heidi* and the Johanna Spyri books set the atmosphere for us. Now the *Little House in the Big Woods* and all of Laura Ingalls Wilder's books, or Meindert de Jong's *Shadrach* and *Wheel on the School* will do the same for you.

The present generation is blessed with a wealth of excellent juvenile books. Here are riches from which to choose that will provide golden pleasure in the present and build strong character for the future. An educator I know says that adults read to find out what others think, while children read to find out what they themselves believe. From her experience with students of high school age she has found that the young people with ideals and principles, with standards of right and wrong, come from homes where reading together is basic to the family pattern. Through the process of identifying and suffering with the characters in their books, children tend to become like those admired.

Of course reading aloud must not be limited to the bed-time hour and to one child at a time. If this great pleasure has been crowded out of your family schedule, to begin you may have to make a festive occasion of reading together. Choose an evening when the television program is dull, start a good book with the dessert, let the best reader do most of the reading, but let each around the table have a turn. On this subject, one grandmother said: "I have nineteen grand-children. They will leave radio or television any time to hear me read aloud. They get tired of second-rate programs the same as grownups do. And besides, it is impersonal enter-tainment. They love the companionship that comes from sharing a book." The family that reads together stays to-gether.

This deep appreciation and fervor for the pages of a story-book is the best way to teach children to read well them-selves. Recently I heard a paper written for a Master's de-gree in education on the subject "Reading for Comprehen-sion." There was not one word in it about the joy of read-ing, about wanting to read on to see what happens next. It sounded as if reading were a dull labor, a bore that must be endured. Oh no, it is all the members of the family experi-encing together delight in Mole and Ratty, Roo and Kanga, Uncle Analdus and Mother Rabbit who was such a worrier, Ola and Einar swapping all their belongings from pencils to cows, Jo and Beth given immortality again with rereading, and on and on, remembered hours of tranquil bliss. Mother can really come to be an authority on at least one type of modern literature, to the enrichment of herself and all her family.

From that reading there will spring up a family language. The more experiences, words, anecdotes, jokes the family have in common, the closer they are bound together. In their patter will be phrases from the books all the family have loved. Any good time is "Song and dance and a gay life, tiddledy pom." Almost anyone, now and then, has the "brain of Pooh." Someone who is feeling sorry for herself is "Eyore." Someone who is boasting a little too freely is "Mr. Toad." Anyone who has so much to do she doesn't know where to begin is "the old sailor my grandfather knew."

There will also be made-up words like "youngered" or "couth and heveled." There are inherited expressions that are worth cherishing. Our great-great-grandmother always said: "Nothing so handy as disappointment"; and "Do as you please and live the longer." So do we. "Oh the shame of it all" spoken with a light touch, releases tense situations in another family. Humor is one of those spiritual values which will help tide us over the years when the children are young. But that is stopping short of the truth, for humor and gaiety and merriment are a never-failing benediction.

4. *Martha and Mary*

"A WOMAN NAMED Martha received him into her house. And she had a sister called Mary, who sat at the Lord's feet and listened to his teaching. But Martha was cumbered with much serving; and she went to him and said, 'Lord, do you not care that my sister has left me to serve alone? Tell her then to help me.' But the Lord answered her, 'Martha, Martha, you are anxious and troubled about many things; one thing is needful. Mary has chosen the good portion, which shall not be taken away from her.'"

This is a mere incident that took place as Jesus and his disciples "went on their way." It was not told as a parable. It is not a principle that Jesus taught, saying, "Let them that have ears, hear." This was a bit of eldering done to fit an individual case. It wasn't that Martha worked and got the meals on the table that was all wrong; it was that she was anxious and troubled. And it is not that the meals do not need to be prepared; it is just that Martha needs to be partly Mary and put first things first.

The incident might even have been reported in this fashion: A woman named Martha received him into her house. And she had a sister called Mary, who worried and could not center herself. She sat at the Lord's feet and questioned him and wearied him with much talking. But Martha was calm and sweet-tempered and went about her work preparing the meal with much serenity. Mary said, "Lord, do you not care that my sister has left us alone? Call her then to come and talk with us." But the Lord answered, "Mary, Mary, you are anxious and troubled about your libido, about your dreams, about the progress of your soul. You waste my time, your time, and that of everyone you meet. One thing is needful, and Martha has chosen that good portion. She has accepted herself, and the frame in which she lives. She is receptive of grace and truth. She has learned to love and serve God and her neighbor as herself. This shall not be taken away from her."

So far as we know, Mary and Martha were two unmarried sisters. Nevertheless to most married women, the connotation suggests that Martha "being cumbered" is one of us. If as Ruysbroeck says in *The Sparkling Stone,* "The love of God is an indrawing and outpouring tide," it is not a case of being either Mary or Martha but of being both. The idea that Martha and Mary balance each other and form a complete whole can open a new world of thought to a wife and mother. If the balance is kept between recreation and being "work-brittle" we may, instead of feeling martyred, be able to smile and say, "Blessed be drudgery."

A modern woman doing a fine piece of teaching and many good works, was advised by her psychiatrist to go home and bake bread, or at least perform some tangible and creative homely work.

Those monasteries which have had the most lasting influence were usually patterned after the order of Saint Benedict, where equal emphasis was laid on work, study, and prayer. "In its greatest representatives, the rhythm of adoration and work is seen in an accentuated form. These people seldom or never answer to the popular idea of idle contemplatives," Evelyn Underhill says. "They do not withdraw from the stream of natural life and effort, but plunge into it more deeply, seek its heart. They have powers of expression and creation, and use them to the full."[1]

The quality of life Saint Benedict advocated, that of wholeness and completeness, can be found here and there today. It was my privilege to spend a year at Pendle Hill, a Quaker adult school. I felt it was a time of apprenticeship to people who had grown in the life of the spirit, not through straining in one direction, but by maintaining lives of balanced action and prayer. Its directors, the Brintons, happily combined learning, reverence, and downright hard work. Anna Brinton's love of menial labor was known to all Pendle Hillers. And I have heard Howard Brinton say many times as he helped with the dishes, or hacked out honeysuckle, "If I do not work with my hands for a whole day I feel out of balance."

WORK MAY BE HARD OR EASY

"Work," says the dictionary, "is the continuous application of energy toward an end, and it may be hard or easy." And whether it is hard or easy usually depends upon a woman's feeling about the multitudinous, monotonous tasks that confront her each day. She has the opportunity to choose one of the most creative roles in the world, or to exist as a toiling slave forever chained to household drudgery.

Mother Currier felt deeply about this: "Aren't you sorry for women who do not enjoy housework? It's still a question whether it's sadder to be one of those, or sadder to long to have a home to do that in, and be without. Once, many years ago, I tried making a list of blessings and bothers and found five troubles and twenty-six blessings—amazing! It sounds

---

[1] *The Life of the Spirit and the Life of Today* by Evelyn Underhill, p. 54. E. P. Dutton and Company, 1922. Used by permission.

trite but starts one thinking. Our blessings really do pile up, and one of my specials is loving to keep my home—not just 'doing the same old work.' "

Other women who explore this subject advise getting through a dirty job as quickly and efficiently as possible so that time may be had for music and books and civic responsibility. Some say there is less strain in the family atmosphere, more of shared joy, where cooking, or ironing, or plowing is accepted as the work of the day, and people are not rushing to get through to rest. There is often less fatigue where there is no sharp cleavage between work and life. "The most important thing in this busy life is living now—the direct experience," writes a mother of four. "Hands in the dishwater; thank you, Lord, for the dishes, for the warmth, for the helper beside me blowing bubbles into a peanut butter jar!"

Casual remarks are often so much more character-forming than all our carefully thought-out speeches. How deeply we need to be good and whole and honest. I can still see the country kitchen, the brown patterned ironstone ware, and the old aunt who said to the do-less little girl beside her, "I like to wash dishes." No sermon was preached, but those five words summed up a not-to-be-despised way of life.

I used to ask the busy mother of six young children, "Don't you get awfully tired and find you need to rest in the afternoon?" Because her work was the expression of her deep love, and because she had an inner rest so many of us know nothing of—"In Him I live and move and have my being"—she could answer, "Oh, I keep going, and I get my second wind."

Working without haste or sense of pressure was a part of her secret. A friend who came back from spending a vacation on a ranch related that her most enlightening experience of the summer was observing the unhurried and tireless work that seemed to continue all day and far into the night. Work does not wear us out, but an emotional jag of feeling abused and overburdened very quickly produces a "cumbered Martha."

If home tasks and daily chores are performed with joy and love, new beauty is seen. The artist in us sees color and shape. The poet in us awakens and we may find ourselves aware of unexpected rhymes and rhythms. One lovely poem, the writer explained, "just came to me as I dusted." Others who work in this spirit of serenity find that they can write the beautiful words that come to them, even with children and much bustle in the house.

A woman needs this intense appreciation of the beauty of a bowl of apples to be pared, or the shape and grain of wood to be polished, but with it she must keep a sense of detachment, a feeling of sitting loose to possessions. She can have at one and the same time a willingness to let anything go if need arises, and an awareness that nothing can take this moment from her.

SACRAMENTAL QUALITY OF WORK

Early Quakers gave up the outward sacraments because they believed that all of life is sacramental. Stephen Grellet said after he gave up his Catholic practice of partaking of communion and became a Friend that he never ate a mouthful of bread or partook of a glass of cold water without offering a prayer of thanksgiving.

When all work is done to the glory of God, Martha learns from Mary the blessed sacrament of the present moment. This sacramental quality of the life of the household is aptly expressed by a mother who wrote: "I have always remembered how Dr. Neilson at Smith used to read the last chapter of Proverbs in chapel at least once a year: 'Who can find a virtuous woman? for her price is far above rubies. The heart of her husband doth safely trust in her,' and how a respect for the everyday household tasks was gradually instilled in me. Such a respect seems to me essential if a woman is to find any kind of creative satisfaction in her home. The domestic routine is after all the constant background of each day. I have heard women complain—and indeed have done so myself—that a good meal is prepared only to be eaten and over with. But if we really think upon this, perhaps we shall find it symbolic of the fact that life needs always to be replenished, and just when we feel something is achieved, life moves forward and demands more of us."

Such insights may become ever more clear as the years go by. Certainly, Mother Currier made the preparation of food a sacrament. "My children came home bringing other relatives and I did everything alone and became neither fussed nor tired. My secret feeling about preparing a Thanksgiving feast is that it should all be done in a spirit of worship. It isn't stuffing a turkey and peeling onions, and washing celery; it is preparing food to place before people to remind them of all their unearned blessings on this day. Then there's a high joy in having the food my strength and care have produced become a source of strength to those I love. In that way—a mystical thing perhaps—I become part of them."

This feeling of symbolism about all our life and work, can surely bring heaven closer to us each day, as Jesus with his homely parables made the two inseparable.

> Christ talked of grass, and wind, and rain,
>   And fig-trees and fair weather,
> And made it his delight to bring
>   Heaven and the earth together.

He spoke of lilies, vines, and corn,
  The sparrow and the raven,
And words so natural, yet so wise,
  Were on men's hearts engraven:

And yeast, and bread, and flax, and cloth,
  And eggs, and fish and candles;
See how the whole familiar world
  He most divinely handles.[2]

If one feels this sacramental quality in daily living every piece of work can become a consecrated act. It is not too difficult to pray on one's knees as a floor is scrubbed, "Wash me, O Lord, as I wash this floor, wash me and I shall be whiter than snow." Awakening from sleep can be woven into a beginning prayer for the day: "As I stretch my body and limber my joints for the day's tasks, thou O Lord, make my spirit supple and ready to accept whatever the day may bring." Again, a prayer of thanksgiving for the first refreshing cold water of the morning: "As this water cleanses the sleep from my eyes, cleanse thou the sins of selfishness and pride and fear from my being. Pour upon me the water of life." And then in the act of dressing: "Clothe me in the garments of righteousness." Prayers so brief can run through all the day's activities. They can be simple, symbolic, spontaneous, based upon the needs and acts of the day.

A woman who grew old with great grace, despite a life beset with sorrow and struggle, taught me the following brief prayer. She had known it ever since she was a little girl. "Lord, show me myself. Lord, show me thyself."

I do not remember which came first, and perhaps it need not be the same for all. For some it may well be, "Lord, show me myself; let me respect and love my inward man, and

---

[2] By T. T. Lynch in *Inner Light, First Series,* p. 168. The Macmillan Company, 1937.

then I shall be ready for the King of Glory to come in. And in time I shall learn to bow before the inner man in all men." Others must first pray, "Lord, show me thyself." Then, after we have learned to love the Lord God with all our strength and all our might, and have become willing to try to be obedient to him, sensitiveness and appreciation of others and of our own gifts will grow.

WORK IS LOVE MADE MANIFEST

Work with our hands is an instinctive urge that should not be disregarded. All little children want to help sweep and make pies. For our daughters to miss this apprenticeship is perilous. But good groundwork has been laid if they catch from us the attitude toward work so well expressed in *The Prophet*.

> Work is love made visible.
>
> And if you cannot work with love but only with distaste, it is better that you should leave your work and sit at the gate of the temple and take alms of those who work with joy.
>
> For if you bake bread with indifference, you bake a bitter bread that feeds but half man's hunger.
>
> And if you grudge the crushing of the grapes, your grudge distils a poison in the wine.
>
> And if you sing though as angels, and love not the singing, you muffle man's ears to the voices of the day and the voices of the night.[3]

If this be so, even foul jobs can be done with joy, yes, even washing socks and diapers. Saint Francis had to look for a leper to wash in order to show his love for all mankind. In our domestic frame, we learn a measure of the same lesson

---

[3] The lines from *The Prophet* by Kahlil Gibran are here reprinted with the permission of the publisher, Alfred A. Knopf, Inc. Copyright 1923 by Kahlil Gibran; renewal copyright 1951 by Administrators C. T. A. of Kahlil Gibran Estate, and Mary G. Gibran.

with less strain. It is so much easier for us to scrub kitchens and shirt bands for those we love—our beginning step in service to humanity.

"Work is love made visible." And it truly takes the love to make the work good. It may be love of God outflowing in service to others—nursing the sick or building cathedrals. It may be love of people—husband, children, mother, friends, so that clothes are made, houses swept, books written, motivated by warm human love.

It may be love of the beautiful that produces the long hours of work required to write a poem, carve a statue, or keep minute bouquets of flowers freshly arranged. The best work is probably that prompted by all sources of love. The garden so breath-takingly lovely that all who behold say, "Oh, she has a green thumb," in all probability grew out of all these kinds of love. It is planted and weeded for love of God; keeping even a bit of the earth beautiful is a service to him, a loving partnership between God and man. Of course a garden beautiful to behold with flowers of perfect symmetry and marvelous color and overflowing with the fruits of the earth, can also be cultivated for love of sharing its bounties and beauties with family and friends. The work of bending over a hoe, kneeling to transplant, is also a kind of joy of creation, a sense of well-being at having one's hands in the rich loamy soil, one's back wet and hot under the rays of the sun.

All living things are amazingly related. Perhaps it is not a myth that the vibration of birdsong helps bring about the unfolding of green leaf and spring blossom. My farmer neighbor, not an otherworldly soul, told me about the poor man who could not afford to buy a good grade of well-selected hens. He had to be content with culls. Mind, they had been scientifically tested, and they were of no use as layers. This poor man was a man of faith. He talked to those hens; he sang to them, he loved them, even as Saint Francis loved his little sisters, the birds. It may be apocryphal, but here is the end of the story as I heard it. Those culled hens eventually won blue ribbons for their prowess at egglaying!

My favorite example of love deliberately made manifest is the Mother Currier quilt story. Each year as Christmas drew near, her sacramental offering to the Christchild, and the crowning gift of all her many kindnesses of the year, was a quilt, hand-pieced for some baby who otherwise might lack sufficient warm covering. That is not strange, you say, many goodhearted women have taken many stitches to cover the naked. The phrase, love in every stitch, is a common-place one. But Mother Currier was able to plumb an even deeper level, for her discipline was—a loving thought back of every stitch. If any least thought of irritation, or resentment, or ill will in any relationship slipped into her heart, she laid aside her handiwork, until she was calm and serene and loving. No sounding brass or tinkling cymbal was sewed into her stitches to mar a baby's sleep. Who can guess how much more was done unto the least of these, because of the wholeness of her gift.

ALTERNATION

"As the body can live only by inhalation and exhalation, nutrition and evacuation, and so on, and as the mind can flourish only by looking out for sensible material and then elaborating and spiritualizing it; so the soul can live, to be fully normal in normal circumstances, only by a double process, occupation with the concrete and then abstraction from it, and this alternately, on and on. If it has not the latter it will grow earthly and heavy; if it has not the former it will grow empty and hazy."[4]

---

[4] *Selected Letters* by Baron Frederick von Huegel. J. M. Dent and Company.

There must be a rhythm to the life of the individual as there is a rhythm in night and day, summer and winter. Such alternation adds greatly to one's peace of mind, to serene and purposeful living. The alternate periods of absorption with the concrete and quiet meditation away from activity need not be evenly spaced. In some areas of the globe, night and day are fairly balanced. But the Laplanders take their seasons of steady sunshine and alternate months of winter darkness with just as much equanimity as we do the more current rhythm. Lives can be like that.

Alternation by years is a partial answer. Of a certainty there should be more time later on to balance the work of life with recreation and prayer. But when the children are small, a woman especially needs intervals of quiet to be herself and not just a mother. Even for those who are "aware as they go commonly sweeping the stair" and "whose kitchens are warmed by His love and peace" there should be a sacred pause within the framework of each day. I have known four women who found this centering time by getting up at five o'clock, before their families were astir.

Not all are so hardy: some prefer a quiet time at night. Young mothers may find more time for reading when the children are little than ever again seems possible. In the evenings because the children cannot be left alone, and baby sitters are expensive, there are hours when all of Thomas Hardy, or Katharine Mansfield, or the new *Women and Sometimes Men* by Florida Scott-Maxwell, can be enjoyed with more leisure than in college, in a career, or in the demanding committee existence which may come later. If she is wise, and if it can at all be managed, the young mother will take an hour in the afternoon when the children nap, to rest herself bodily and to refresh her spirit with some inspiring bit of reading, be it poetry, the biographies of Mad-

ame Curie, Rufus Jones, Harry Emerson Fosdick, or the letters of Saint Paul.

If it is impossible to achieve a physical separation, even
for a brief time, then the sensible woman will accept this
encompassing, and still find a way out to free her spirit. An
Australian wrote a thank you note for a playpen given after
the birth of her fourth child. "You will never know how I
appreciate the pen. It is a godsend. I sit in it every afternoon and read and the children can't get near me." Another
mother wears a large red bow to indicate her time of withdrawal. The three youngsters feel her presence; they know
they can call for Mother if Jim falls out of the apple tree, or
Bob lets the axe slip, but when that bright red ribbon is
pinned on her blouse nothing short of an emergency will per-
suade these children to violate their mother's withdrawal into
her inner world. She respects her inner self and they respect her.

In her solid Martha days Mary can find time, maybe
while she brushes her hair, for at least a page of some such
book as Oldham's *Devotional Diary,* Fenelon's *Letters to
Women,* Gerald Heard's *Prayers and Meditations,* or Evelyn
Underhill's *Anthology of the Love of God.* Certainly we do
not need great gulps of reading. Lin Yutang says the reason
Americans cannot appreciate Confucius is because we gallop
through a book at one sitting. Instead, he says that we should
ponder one great thought for days. We do not need to be
ashamed that we need books to help us grow in the life of
the spirit. Teresa, the eagle saint, is a comfort. She confessed
that for fourteen years she could never use meditation unless joined with reading.

Books of inspiration should be sifted and tested until those
that speak to one's condition are found. Then, why experiment too widely? An old hand at cooking does with less and

less tries at orange stuffing or eggplants en casserole. She has so many tried and true recipes at her command that life is scarcely long enough to repeat them as often as the family desires. Of course, a new book now and then—just as occasionally a special French dressing or an oatmeal cookie recipe must be garnered, after a neighbor has proved it at her table.

A verse of the Bible memorized and clung to throughout the day can be of steady help. I feel it is the indirect way to influence the unconscious. Martha can make her own short Bible, reading and marking for rereading the passages that come alive to her. Dean Sperry says that no one can do this for you. Sir Wilfred Grenfell read, marked, and made marginal comments on a new Bible each year.

Rereading the Gospels recently I paid special attention to the women who knew Jesus. He treated them as individuals worthy of courtesy and respect, an attitude unique in a day when women were little more than chattels. And yet I do not find that he ever says to one of them in quite the same way that he does to the chosen twelve, "Leave all—all family responsibility, all possessions that are necessary to home life—to follow my way."

His belief in the importance of the family was so great that rather than belittling or diminishing it, Jesus made the family the basis of an all-inclusive, universal concept. God is our Father, and whoever does his will is my brother and sister and mother. Those women who learned of Love's way from Jesus served him. Mary and Joanna and Susanna and many others provided for Jesus and the twelve out of their means. They were faithful stewards of this world's goods. At the crucifixion the Marys and Salome ministered to him. Let us take comfort, all of us who are cumbered, who seem to proceed so slowly, that it was to Martha our Lord said, "I am the resurrection and the life."

5. *Sacred Idleness*

THE CROSS we have used to signify the wholeness of life combines in one piece, prayer and recreation. The Puritans left a heritage that makes us feel guilty about re-creating ourselves through fun and merriment. A century earlier, however, Teresa of Avila, that spiritual giant, that doughty reformer, knew well that recreation must not be neglected. She really meant amusements, for she often danced and sang with her nuns and told them humorous stories. Even more than a saint, a housewife needs time for idle play and time to gain perspective.

It is in the light touch, in whimsicalities, in a sense of the ridiculous that we best see our littleness, see that we are but a seed that needs to lie dormant in the good dark earth of God. Recreation provides the change of rhythm that sends us back refreshed to homemaking and service in the community. Those who never unbend and relax, who strain too eagerly to fly off into the life of the spirit, miss being rooted and grounded in the love of God. The cross is firmly fixed where we begin to be created anew.

Jesus said that a sad countenance was not to accompany fasting. Sidney Smith's advice has become a family maxim in one household: "Never give way to melancholy; resist it steadily, for the habit will encroach. Little pleasures often banish melancholy better than higher and more exalted objects: and no means ought to be thought too trifling which can oppose it either in ourselves or in others."[1]

The little pleasure might be a new hat, or a pan of rolls baked for the next-door neighbor. Evelyn Underhill in speaking of creaturely enjoyments that preserve balance said: "Remember Saint Francis with his love of birds and music, sun and air; Saint Teresa's eau-de-cologne; Ruysbroeck's and Saint Bernard's passion for the forest. As to what you say about the cloistered life, I don't know whether you have ever known any nuns or monks personally. I know a good many and as a matter of fact, they live the life of the senses just as much as anyone else, only in a peculiarly simple and detached way. If you want to find the person who combines spiritual passion with appreciation of a cup of coffee—go to a convent. It is just there you find this type of perfection."[2]

Leisure is an attitude of mind and spirit. The modeling of clay that is a hobby for one may be a business of ceramics to another. I feel certain we must learn again to participate as we seek renewal, rather than depend upon spectator amusements. It is participation in creation that re-creates and gives release from tenseness and overseriousness.

"Work is not always required of a man. There is such a thing as a sacred idleness, the cultivation of which is now fearfully neglected."[3] What idleness is more wholesome than being in the company of a few kindred spirits gaining enlargement of vision, fresh insights, knowledge that gives courage with which to face our times? The test of worth is,

---

[1] *Memoirs of Sidney Smith* by Lady Holland. Harper and Brothers, 1855.

[2] *Letters of Evelyn Underhill*, edited by Charles Williams, pp. 78-79. Longmans, Greene and Company, 1943. Used by permission.

[3] *George Macdonald Anthology* by C. S. Lewis, p. 109. The Macmillan Company, 1947. Used by permission.

if the participant leaves with a lift of spirit, a radiance gained that adds glow to all the rest of the week.

CREATIVE READING GROUPS

There is creative reading as well as creative writing. And the proverb says: "He that would bring home the wealth of the Indies, must carry out the wealth of the Indies."

At the age of thirty-five I had my first experience of moving to a new town where there was no old friend or relative to include me in an established social group. Why strangers, for self-interest if not for purposes of worship, do not more often attend the most promising church in their new community, I have never been able to fathom. At any rate, our family wanted a church home. After we took the initiative of attending Sunday services, church members began to call.

One older neighbor said, "My good friend and I get together once a week to read. Would you care to join us? We've sometimes enjoyed biography; just now we have finished Nehru's *Toward Freedom* and are about to begin Gunther's *Inside Latin America*. Do come next Friday."

That reading group was a precious adventure in friendship through an objective interest. Friendships in the making need a common bond, be it "shop talk," gardening or other hobbies, politics, sports, or insights gained through a new book. I would not belittle our common humanity, and am inclined to agree with Katharine Butler Hathaway[4] that the only things that are really important to talk about are such things as marrying and dying and God. Still those fundamentals of life are apt to be an achievement in the realm of communication rather than a beginning. Without a shared interest it is too easy to drop into talk of personalities, and then still lower into gossip. Caring about people is essential,

4 In *The Little Locksmith*. Coward-McCann, 1943.

and gossip can be golden. Yet the malicious sort is such a common tendency that few exist who do not need the "whatsoever things are true, honest, and lovely" to lift them above talebearing and detraction.

Our shared book was a bridge out of easy ruts on to new highways of thought. From being current-minded with Gunther, we became curious to see how the Jewish Franz Werfel would write the story of a Catholic saint, so we read *The Song of Bernadette*. There were five of us now, Methodist, Presbyterian, Quaker, and one an unaffiliated spiritual descendant of Abou Ben Adhem. Theological discussions and heart-searchings abounded. In talking of the miracles at Lourdes two of us kept referring to Alexis Carrol's *Man the Unknown*. We all thought we should like to read it together. So many writers, Rufus Jones and Fosdick among others, referred to Carrol as a scientist who backed their statements on faith, that we sought answers in his great knowledge. We did not really find them; he seemed to come so close, and then to turn back sharply, basing the hope of the world on more science, more synthesis of knowledge. But in a way he gave us an answer, for we felt the humility of this learned man. We read slowly; there seemed to be so much to talk about.

The other two books I remember well were *The Little Locksmith* by Katharine Butler Hathaway—the beauty of her language and the beauty of her spirit—and Dr. Oliver's book entitled *Fear*. The books were helpful, but the experience of hours of peace spent together is the stronger memory now.

Such little groups of friends, reading and sewing together, yes, and eating simple food together, can create small oases of love. They can act as a spring of refreshment and vitality in a world dried and embittered by the winds of distrust and fear.

Poets Walk In

But once more we moved. And again heart's ease was found in a creative reading and writing group that came to be known by the sign of welcome upon the front door, "Poets Walk In." On first and third Tuesday afternoons we who opened the door walked in, to beauty and delight and imagination and love. We left outside the unfinished ironing, the unsolved budget, our mundane cares. Here for two hours we would not "look before or after, or pine for what is not, but live in the holy carelessness of the eternal now."

Penn had his *holy experiment* and we "poets" have ours. How did it happen? One of the "three great ladies up the valley" in Vermont came to Germantown to spend the winter. Robert Frost calls her "saint, poet, and reformer." We were to find out about the first and last qualities, but we were well aware that she was a poet. We had all read her famous quatrain:

> The golf links lie so near the mill
> That almost every day
> The laboring children can look out
> And see the men at play.

Why not form a little circle around Sarah Cleghorn to read poetry?

We went that first time with our anthologies and clippings. Poems of Shelley and Keats, Frost and Santayana were read, a little haltingly and a little questioningly. Some of us had not read aloud since school days; we wondered too if our favorites appeared queer to others. Many that first afternoon were strangers to each other.

I don't remember about the second and third afternoons, except that each time that door was opened the sense of expectancy and adventure and pleasure was heightened. But very early in the history of this group Sally, as we all lov-

ingly came to call her, read us Masefield's "The Everlasting
Mercy." To recall the beautiful reading of those beautiful
words is to be lifted up all over again.

The poets grew, in wisdom, we hope; certainly in joy, for
pleasure shared is always multiplied; and in numbers, for
each of us knew and brought along a friend or two whose
delight was poetry. Our pleasant golden room was filled. A
hall or a church parlor would not have the cozy carefree-
ness of these easy chairs before an open fire. Furthermore,
the trust and intimacy that permits the secret essential self
to be laid forth bare in a poem, might not continue if the
group grew beyond twenty. By this time, nearly every other
meeting was given over to the original verse of the members. But good things must grow. There can't be limitations
to any experience as renewing as this, I kept feeling. And
then I knew it was I who must fall to the ground and die,
must split off from the parent cell. Does this sound over-
dramatic? It is tragedy to leave people who love you, and
want you, and include you as a poet even when all you ever
have written or ever will write is "promes." (Promes are
neither good straightforward prose, nor the singing, sug-
gestive words of poetry.)

Still it was I who had the concern. It was I who traveled
the greatest distance. Surely there must be a dozen women
in my own immediate neighborhood who would be just as
transformed by entering an open door of poetry into the
wealth of the Indies.

Believing that breaking bread together feeds the spirit as
well as the body, and knowing that tea late in the afternoon
may spoil a woman's disposition for preparing a bountiful
supper, I asked my New Jersey friends to bring their own
sandwiches and come to a poetry party. This we continued
to do, gathering around a long table at one o'clock, to talk
and laugh and eat our own bread and cheese, or carrots and

apples if we were inclined to be somewhat "Pooh Bear" shaped, and drink coffee, or occasionally tea. Always it was iced tea in the summer when we sat out under the big old elm and watched the goldfinches and orioles more than we listened to words describing nature.

A letter from one of the group says what can happen to people who do not neglect to cultivate the art of sacred idleness: "Ever since last week there has been the urge to write a brief note and say how nice the afternoon was. I was so farm-weary and farm-possessed, that it was good to see all of you and have Jane's poem start a new line of thought. I spent the evening copying poems and thinking possible thoughts for new ones and had my mind completely removed from corn and the weather!" I believe this experience, personal and collective, can be duplicated over and over.

Prayer Cells

Less unusual than poetry clubs are cell groups and retreats, which with a steady osmotic quality are emerging in the world today. Valuable books for inspiration and instruction in quickening such experiments into life are Elton Trueblood's *Alternative to Futility* and Douglas Steere's *Time to Spare*. Friends who had attended a conference on psychology twenty-five years ago felt many questions were unanswered. They had learned to clean the drains ("When the unclean spirit has gone out of a man, it goes and brings in seven other spirits more wicked than itself, . . . and they enter in and dwell there"), but not how to let the unconscious be a wellspring of the water of life.

A regular gathering where the time should be divided between silent meditation and discussion of common problems was the beginning of an answer. The informal and fluid character of this fellowship has been its strength. A small plain committee room of a meetinghouse has been the set-

ting. The original members have brought other seekers and
lonely people. Those who gained little from a half hour or
more of silent worship, or who were swept up into a more
active life, dropped out. Some have come faithfully every
two weeks; some intermittently as household duties lighten
or tensions become too great to bear alone. One member said
at one time, "This group means more to me than church; I
wouldn't miss it for anything." Having since found greater
joy and strength in her own Sunday worship, she said recently with equal sincerity, "The amazing thing is, any of
us can stay away for two months or two years, and return
with the same sense of belonging and the same warm welcome."

The members of this meditation group have spoken not
only of their common problems—dying, growing, and finding
God—but also of how they pray. Is there, for instance, a limit
to those for whom intercessory prayer may be offered? One
shared her conviction that to be channels of redemptive love
we must truly belong to the order of the towel and basin.
"If I do not wash you, you have no part in me." They have
in turn presented their favorite saints and books that have
been significant to them. They have read aloud together psychological studies such as *The Open Way* and *Creation Continues*. Mark's Gospel provoked so much discussion that only
a few verses could be covered at each meeting.

The halting, slow reading that results as a book is passed
around the circle has merit. Since most people are more eye-
minded than ear-minded, it is better if each member has a
book to follow, as turns are taken reading aloud. If concen-
tration of thought were the main object, a solitary reader
settled in her own quiet corner might comprehend more, but
I doubt it, since ideas that sink into our beings through several senses have a more lasting influence.

Besides, mental stimulation is not primary, but a hand-in-hand adventuring with companionship. Intellectual and spiritual concepts are heightened as friendship is deepened. Whatever is read with interest and delight and imagination, be it current events, poetry, biography, or soul's journey, brings kinship. There is as much varied subject matter as there are many ways of reading; all can be good. A common bond and a mutual participation set in a framework of sacred idleness are bound to result in joyful fellowship.

The American Scholar is educated by nature, by books, by action, by his duties, Emerson said. Even "creative reading" of other men's books must be kept in balance, he preached. When a friend writes, "If only you knew how much it means to me to be one of the group! I've been 'starved' the last two years and didn't know it," she does not mean she has been without books but has been without creative fellowship. She had been cut off from kindred spirits with whom she could discuss ideas and in whose company her own independent thinking found nourishment. I believe the joy of a group reading aloud together can be the very bread of life. This intangible substance by which we are sustained is the "wealth of the Indies we finally carry home"—the fellowship of love.

LEISURE TO DO WHAT YOU LIKE

Pleasure in creative reading groups, however, would not be the open-sesame to all weary women. A mother of three children between the ages of six and twelve, defined leisure as doing the things you love to do. We have come to think of it as spare time, being without occupation, but the root meaning has to do with being free. "It is lawful; it is permitted." Leisure allows us to do the things we want to do. To sew for days and days and close her eyes to dust and fingermarks was the way that particular mother became re-created.

She admitted though that dressmaking had taken on a new delight when she enrolled for an all-day sewing course that met once a week; there she had such a stimulating experience being in the company of other women who were also being instructed that she went home exhilarated. She said, "It was easy to become stagnant alone; with all the group learning together I felt young and lighthearted. You don't worry about your children while you are learning."

Whether it is learning alone or in fellowship with others will depend upon what is needed by the individual. Evelyn Underhill was constantly reminding those who wanted "to go faster than grace" to alternate their devotions with light novels and warm milk; to develop an interest in geology, music, weaving, some exercise of mind or body quite at the opposite pole from prayer and meditation.

Returning from a visit to the Kentucky Mountains where the women still weave bedspreads and piece quilts, a friend of mine expressed her belief that the dearth of love many young couples feel for their homes stems from failure to create tangible demonstrations of that love. The present trend of "Do it yourself" is probably one evidence in the right direction. How can a home reflect the personality of the people who live there if an interior decorator has chosen all the color combinations and all the materials and styles?

Perhaps the despair and purposelessness in many today is the fruit of what was considered by the medieval church one of the greatest sins, *Acedia*. Chaucer says, "Acedia is a compound of depression, sloth, and irritability, which plunges the whole man into a lazy languor and works in him a constant bitterness." The irritable, do-less, depressed woman is often miserable because she has not found the joy of creating. And not only is she miserable but all her family suffer because of her. If we are made in the image of our Creator, it surely means that we too should always be creating.

Thirty thousand years ago, in the caves of Lascaux in France, human beings began to find a way of worship and to record that search as they painted their legends, their dreams, their hopes. These early creative expressions are known as the Cradle of Man's Art. So long a search for personal and collective fulfillment through the medium of art would seem to justify our continued efforts to find recreation through drawing and painting, no matter how primitive. One woman's grief was assuaged as she arose each sleepless dawn, and without disturbing her family went softly to the basement where she could paint her sorrow away.

The results of creativity need not always have visible shape and design. The main field of creativity in our day, Fritz Kunkel once said, should be human relationships. Listening to a neighbor can create friendship; listening to a bird can create worship; listening to God can create a soul.

Our minds need many kinds of exercise, and creativity which uses mind and muscles is a source of balance and a wellspring of joy. A woman who walks in the woods, who makes a lampshade, who bakes a loaf of bread, who refinishes an old chair, has not time for bitterness and depression. Acedia may be the aching of an unused faculty. Handmade curtains can give enough character to a home to redeem the hotchpotch of furniture with which a young couple must get along. How fortunate is a woman who is able to make love visible through her fingers and thus deserve being called a handmaiden of the Lord.

Extreme preoccupation with household projects may cause us to feel guilty about taking time out to enjoy the beauty of creation not of our own making. Eight-year-old Karen said that her mother was nice and pretty until she got her speed up! And Karen's mother looking back on those tense, overbusy days, probably suffered as did the writer of "Lost October."

> There never comes a day like this, all gold
> And shining like a bubble in the sun,
> But I recall the afternoon I told
> You I'd no time for play: work must be done!
> Work must be done, and there the gold day wasted,
> And there the mellowness of earth and sky
> And leaf and air went hour by hour untasted
> For scruples sown too well in such as I!
>
> And then October's brightness faded, turning
> Her dear enchantment into dull November,
> And setting in my brain one question burning:
> Now what can I, now what can I remember
> Of work I bent above that day, until
> It was too late to climb the golden hill![5]

THE GOOD ARE THE MERRY

When one young mother of five stair-step children begins to feel sorry for herself, or assumes a noble look-how-I-sac-rifice-for-you expression, her husband rushes up with a kiss and pins on her the "martyr button." Because men are often more objective, and more easily see the funny side of trouble-some situations, we who are apt to be a little tense and over-serious should thank the good Lord for the male perspective that can laugh off our mountains into their proper molehill dimensions. We who are blessed with husbands and sons are often freed from "varm" (the opposite of charm) by such sane and loving words as "Dinna fash thyself, woman." In the Scots Bible, Jesus' eldering of Martha seems said in just such a spirit. When she was "unco pernickity aboot

---

[5] By Elaine V. Emans in *Good Housekeeping,* October, 1936, p. 19.

mickle service" and asking Jesus to bid her sister help, he
replies, "Martha, Martha, ye are put-till't and fashed wi' a
hantle o' things."

Mother Currier once sent me sound advice when she
sensed that I was "put-till't and fashed wi' a hantle of
things." "If you could once make up your mind in the fear
of God never to undertake more of work of any sort than
you can carry on calmly, quietly, without hurry or flurry,
and the instant you feel yourself growing nervous and like
one out of breath, would stop and take breath, you would
find this simple common-sense rule doing for you what no
prayers or tears could ever accomplish."[6]

If we do not learn by ourselves or from our family and
friends, we may be able to learn from the psychiatrist. In a
study of chronic fatigue, Dr. Kepler of the Mayo Clinic
emphasized four factors that should constantly influence our
lives: play, love, work, and worship. No single one of these
should be allowed to dominate at the expense of another.
Play, he insisted, has a far more vital effect on mind and
body than most people dream as it releases the creative im-
pulses and is a safety valve for the emotions. For these insights on the importance of balance in normal lives and the
necessity of restoring balance in sick people, Dr. Kepler
gives full credit to a book written in 1914 by Richard C.
Cabot, *What Men Live By:* Play, Work, Love, Worship.
(The theme of this book indicates how much I too am in-
debted to Dr. Cabot.)

The cheerfulness of the Chinese people impressed George
N. Kates during the seven years that he spent studying
their ancient culture:

I believe that the underlying philosophy of Chinese life
bears with it a conviction that simple cheerfulness is—by all

---

[6] *Life and Letters of Elizabeth Prentiss.* Randolph, 1882.

odds and under all circumstances—the most sensible and the wisest attitude for anything that may befall. The smile of good humor, though, must really come from within. Why be haughty, or arrogant, or tense, or morose, when everything in the world runs so much better if one will only take it easily and in good part, and then enjoy the amusement and cheer? This lesson has been well learned. Laughter springs up of itself; at times the gaiety is infectious.[7]

Everywhere, a cheerful perspective and a sense of fun can free people from hardness of heart and stiffness of neck. Perhaps such counsel sounds like mere common sense. Then it should be stressed that common sense and nonsense do assist growth in the life of the spirit. Hilarity and daftness save us from taking ourselves too seriously. Saint Teresa's sparkling sense of humor matched her deep inward joy. "God preserve us from gloomy saints," she was fond of saying. What if we were to sing "Grimly, grimly, we adore thee." Our "joy is the grace we say to God." Let us trust Sir Richard Grenfell's advice: "About the religious life divorced from common sense, I believe as Betsy Prig about Mrs. 'Arris, "There ain't no sich person.'"

---

[7] *The Years That Were Fat* by George N. Kates, p. 165. Harper and Brothers, 1952. Used by permission.

+

6.   *Mercy Has a Human Heart*

> For Mercy has a human heart;
>   Pity, a human face;
> And Love, the human form divine:
> And Peace, the human dress.
> —*William Blake*

THE TENDER CARE that parents give their children is akin to the love of God for his children. But a good thing like mother love may become corrosive if it is possessive and ingrown. A mother's love needs to grow to include all the children of the world. The wonderful paradox is that while our children are not ours, but the children of life, all the world needs a bit of mothering.

Parents care for the souls of their children, but they have to begin by cleaning up their messes. And as long as we live, God does not seem to want us to abandon cleaning up the messes of the children of the world. Jesus washed his disciples' feet and Francis bathed the lepers, graphic reminders to us never to cut ourselves off from ministering to the world's creaturely needs.

THE LEAST OF THESE

People with potential abilities as volunteers often do not know where to begin to be useful. I wish I might give them encouragement for I know well the inward and outward difficulties of becoming a responsible volunteer. Twenty years ago a teacher of one of our children mentioned that once or twice each week she visited in a nearby hospital. At first she spent time in the children's ward, telling stories, playing games, leading the children in singing together. She discovered, however, that the little ones did not need her as did the old people. So many of them were afraid to die; so many were sad and lonely. I had no faith that her kind of ministry was anything I was fitted to do. What could I do that would be of any use in a hospital or settlement house?

Then we moved and began to attend a Friends' Meeting. One member reporting on behalf of the social service committee stated that she took magazines each month to the local county jail. This knowledge inspired me to go and do likewise. The magazines were accepted, but my shy inquiry as to whether or not there were some female prisoners who might like to be visited, was brusquely rejected. "Their families come to see them," I was told.

When we moved to another county seat, the massive old gray walls of its fortresslike jail laid a constant shadow on my heart. There, the warden was friendly and grateful to have someone visit the women prisoners. A migrant worker from Florida was indeed far from home and friends. But the girls with nearby families were also bereft, for time was an endless thread that wrapped them round in a blanket of bleakness. It was simple to carry them magazines, books, materials for sewing and embroidery. It is difficult to imagine what a new face, friendly everyday conversation, and a willingness to listen mean to people who possess nothing but time.

Most wardens of county jails and superintendents of state reformatories welcome visitors whether they come as members of an organization or on an individual mission. Otherwise many prisoners have no one to come see them! When I asked Miss Mahan, head of the New Jersey State Reformatory, for advice about visiting she said, "Just remember that prisoners are people. Talk with them—and listen—as you would with any other person."

At Framingham, Massachusetts, where the state reformatory is located, the women in the surrounding communities are well established as Friendly Visitors. Any girl who wishes may have an unsupervised visit from her special friend once a month, and in between visits she may receive letters, magazines, and small gifts. The visitors also stand ready to assist with those on day parole or on release from the institution.

A similar group is at work at the State Home for Girls in Trenton, New Jersey. Often it is merely a matter of awareness, of openness to all of life which proves to be the starting point of such projects. So it was for three Philadelphia Quakers who initiated the concern for the girls in the Trenton Home. After hearing Helen Bryan speak of her experiences inside the Federal Institution for Women at Alderson, West Virginia,[1] they were led to ask questions, read pertinent material, attend conferences on penology, and visit in correctional institutions. Their next step was to spend three days at the reformatory at Framingham observing, talking with the girls, learning from Dr. Miriam Van Waters, superintendent of that progressive institution, where women become truly penitent and do reform. They came away filled with enthusiasm for the possibilities of service and as a result the Friendly Visitors are now active at the Trenton State Home.

One of them, describing the Framingham visit, told this

---

[1] See *Inside* by Helen R. Bryan.

story about a meeting of the prison literary club. Dr. Van Waters had read from one of Bishop Sheen's books, and then went around the circle asking each girl what was her idea of love. Most of them spoke exclusively of earthly affections until it came the turn of a young woman, the mother of two small boys, who insisted, "Oh, it is so much more than men and women's desire for each other, or even parents' caring for their children. Love is divine, it is that which makes us grow. I was rebellious when I was sent here; I was rebellious at the length of time I had to stay; but now I see how necessary it was for me to have time to think and so begin to change."

God so loved the world that he sent his Son that we might learn about love through personality. Most of us are doubting rebels and unless like Thomas we can put our hands into the hands of our Lord, we will not believe. Dr. Van Waters had put her hand into the hand of that girl and her trust had redeemed her.

The imaginative love that redeems people in barren situations may be found in a professional worker, in an organized group of volunteers, or in a pioneering individual. Because of a term of jury service a friend of mine in New York State got interested in penal reform. That general interest led her to a particular girl indicted on a charge of forgery. Kate welcomed the visits of the friendly woman who came once each week bringing magazines and sewing materials. And in turn, Kate was glad to give the embroidered towels and blankets to nearby Negro migrants about whom my friend had long been concerned. A letter describes a visit of their choir to the county jail: "I am so grateful to the migrant singers who truly became our friends, and wiped away what remained of the racial barrier. I wish you could have heard the prayer their leader said in the jail the day they sang there. It almost made me weep." These individuals, ministering to each other through imaginative planning, handicraft, and music, became bound together in the bundle of life.

We need to feel that in the sight of God if not before an earthly judge the difference between the sins of those who run afoul the law and our sins is slight. It is love for Christ that sends us to those locked behind prison bars. "Lord, when did we see thee . . . sick or in prison and visit thee?"

Why is it we are so afraid of being kind? We fear being classed as Lady Bountifuls or Do-gooders; we fear a psychological analysis of our motives; we fear we are rationalizing some manifestation of the ego. All motives are mixed. We can only offer our motives to God, saying humbly, "I know that this deed will give me satisfaction; I know that if I were my neighbor I would appreciate his coming to see me; I know that our Lord told us we were his disciples if we loved and served one another. Take my motives, Lord, and use them for thy glory and the welfare of all thy children." And having laid this burden of painful inquiry upon the Comforter, even the Spirit of Truth and Love, let us set forth to be lovingly useful.

The Lonely Old

A young mother describes how she came to start one Golden Age Club. As she called from house to house collecting for the annual community chest drive, many older men and women asked about the welfare of neighbors whom they had not seen for months. She saw the need for a central meeting place and carried her idea to the ministers and the priest, to the mayor, the doctors, the merchants, the housewives, enlisting their help. They rallied around her, raised money, secured a club room and enrolled drivers to transport the members. It has been a fine experience for everybody. The members of this club like to learn new skills: to weave, to cane chairs, to paint and refinish old furniture, to make and repair toys. They love to give their time and their skills and their handicraft to others. They put on plays and give entertainments for veterans at the nearby hospital. And now once again these old neighbors find life pleasant and worthwhile.

At last I became ready to serve the lonely old ones. Having moved away from the shadow of the county jail, and reasonably close to the Philadelphia Center for Older People, I was ready to accept an invitation to serve on its board. It seemed a good thing for a board member to work also as a volunteer. The director asked what skill I had to offer. Could I direct the sewing group or teach a craft? Could I lead the current events club? No, but I like poetry! But nobody has ever asked for any kind of literary club.

It is now six years since the members of the Center were invited to a poetry party. There sitting in a great circle each person in turn introduced himself, telling something of his childhood and sharing a poem or song of days gone by. After each had contributed, it was suggested that all of those who had enjoyed this form of entertainment, who loved poetry and reading aloud, might like to form a poetry club. "When should we begin, and how often should we meet?" They answered, "Right away and every week."

And so these old folks come to our meetings from all over the city and its suburbs. The first summer only four or five might appear. But often we had our best meetings when the group was small enough to be quite intimate and informal. Now twenty or more meet regularly to read childhood favorites by Longfellow, Helen Hunt Jackson, J. P. Curran; to take to our hearts new authors such as Margaret Lloyd, Esther Wood, Phyllis McGinley; to sing spirituals; to share our own original verse. Everyone participates and we end

with tea, and jokes, and the Mizpah benediction. Poetry and
laughter and worship bring us into close fellowship.

Why do they come? For companionship of course; for
the opportunity to take an active part each time; for the
satisfaction in having an audience respond with pleasure
to their offerings whether original or not. They come too
because they really love poetry. This older generation, who
can still quote long passages from the Bible, who have many
fine old poems stored away in their minds, should shake
modern educators out of the theory that children are not
to be taught to memorize what they do not fully understand. Poetry, through its music and rhythm and beauty,
feeds the soul of young and old. The McGuffey Readers and
Spellers of old were interspersed with good poetry. It became a part of these people. Now in their later years they
are glad of a place wherein they are reminded to turn again
to the inspiration that was learned in childhood.

Since the reading of poetry has proved to be a healing
therapy for mentally disturbed patients, perhaps "golden
hours of poetry clubs" such as ours help to keep older people
sane and serene.

The members like their "teacher" to visit them. They may
want to show me quilts and treasures made with their hands;
they may be glad of my admiration for the plants in the
windows; they may set a banquet table and serve fried butter fish in the middle of the afternoon; they may just be
glad of a listening ear. At times seated in one of their bleak
little rooms I find myself hearing the long story of a life
filled with high adventure or the attainment of crucial responsibility. Every life is a book and I, having observed
the end of the story, am now because of my love and respect
for my old friends taken by the hand and led back to the
beginning of the tale.

The Sick

When old people fall sick and are placed in hospital or nursing home, the only touch with the outside world, the only break in the monotony of their days, may come from the visits of a volunteer leader or the other members of their Golden Age Club.

Of all pitiable creatures, the most hopeless are those in nursing homes which are financed solely with the patients' public assistance checks. These sick and lonely old ones need exactly the same kind of loving attention and appreciation that small children need who are without a security of love. If only there could be a regular friendly visitor for every one of these deserted souls who feel bereft and without hope!

From the institutional point of view the need for volunteer help is greater than ever. Fifty years ago, for instance, hospitals were highly endowed, nurses were available, funds were adequate to pay all workers. Now money is scarce, nurses are scarce, institutions are actually dependent upon nurse's aids, Grey Ladies, Pink Ladies.

Volunteers are needed in hospital nurseries to sit and hold the babies while they have their bottles. It is well known that infants in institutions do not thrive because they lack what the overworked nurses call TLC. Tender loving care cannot be put in a capsule, but it can be given by a warmhearted woman who loves holding babies.

A friend of mine who longed for the role of motherhood has turned her maternal yearning and kindergarten training into play therapy with the children in a big city hospital. Instead of continuing to say, "If only I had a houseful of children," she is now happy with a hospital full of children. My friend admits that the children needed more attention than the busy nurses could give, but she goes on to say,

"They did not need me as I needed them. Now my days are filled with a purpose."

DUE-NESS

The new time that becomes ours when the children are of school age allows us to make the love learned inside the home manifest outside the home. That does not mean that a mother should be involved day after day in volunteer activities. Until the children are in college, or homes of their own, perhaps community service should be limited to one afternoon a week. It does mean that a woman should take stock of herself when the youngest child is off to school.

Will she eventually become one of the bored and restless women who lie abed late, make their morning coffee and newspapers last until noon, and spend their afternoons drinking cocktails to kill time? Or will she become one of the 45 per cent of middle-aged women who take jobs, not primarily from lack of money but from lack of imagination? Or will she find a need to which she can give herself? Besides bringing up two adopted children, one woman I know has given active leadership to League of Women Voters and Young Women's Christian Association. In her cynical moments she claims that women take jobs in order to shut their eyes and hearts to the unending community and personal needs.

If she begins early to be open to adventures of service, a mother need never fear middle and old age. One gracious and charming older woman began while she was still a young mother to make the causes of peace, prohibition, and politics her own. She said that she was fortifying herself for the day when her children would be grown and gone.

American women are the most fortunate women of any age or culture. We have both opportunity to do what we want to do, and leisure in which to do it. Our houses are filled with laborsaving devices. Our husbands are the most considerate in history. Having been blessed with strength, with skills, with education, with happiness, how else can a oneness with creation be preserved unless those of us who have too much, share with those who have too little. Such a sharing is "love's lovely duty." All service should be undertaken in that spirit, or if it is too hard to separate duty from a grim self-righteousness then let us create a new word and say it should be undertaken from a sense of dueness. We owe so much because we have received so freely.

For years my Jewish neighbor went each week to read to a blind student at Temple University. Later she became a volunteer at the Norristown State Mental Hospital. Every week she took a small group of women to walk who otherwise would have had no outing, no chance for friendly talk with a normal person. Since maid service freed my neighbor from household tasks, she felt an obligation to serve others less privileged than herself. The Council of Jewish Women encourages their members to give time regularly as volunteers. Many Jewish women staff well-baby clinics, act as assistants to teachers of retarded children, sew for relief, learn Braille in order to make transcriptions, and work in other areas of need.

A recent German emigree threw herself into all facets of American life. After a visit to her native land, she became convinced that henceforth the United States was to be her spiritual as well as legal home. The thing she missed most in Europe was a willingness to spend oneself on social and community enterprise. No initiative seemed to exist for undertaking volunteer work.

Girl Scouts, 4-H Clubs, Young Women's Christian Association, Sunday schools, all need leaders who will work with young people to keep life sound and decent. Some women will turn their energies to needed legislation. Some will

serve on boards and committees. But some of us must seek
out the lonely and forsaken, the wretched and broken-down.

Old age, physical limitations, and mental illnesses as well
as moral lapses confine people to institutional life. Nearly
all have too much time and too little love. Such lonely
people long for a love that manifests itself in providing work,
hobbies, leadership, and friendliness.

It takes one kind of courage to meet misfortunes that come
to you. It takes courage of another kind to go out and in-
volve yourself in troubles that would never touch you if
you remained cloaked in indifference. Even hate is more
akin to love than indifference. It is a more grievous sin to
do nothing, to bury the one talent we have, than to fail
occasionally. Our hearts grow hard if we live with indifference, without compassion, without sensitiveness to need,
without any feeling of membership one with another.

> For Mercy, Courage, Kindness, Mirth,
> There is no measure upon earth.
> Nay, they wither, root and stem,
> If an end be set to them.
> Overbrim and overflow,
> If your own heart you would know;
> For the spirit born to bless
> Lives but in its own excess.
>
> —*Lawrence Binyon*

Some people are afraid that the pleasure of making others
happy is but an inverted kind of selfishness. We moderns
have grown afraid that warmheartedness is a mother complex and that kindly deeds are a form of self-indulgence.
That no motives are ever crystal-clear needs emphasis. Most
things are done for many reasons. Jesus did not agonize
over motives of service nor attempt to explain the mystery
of pain and suffering. He set about to open men's eyes that

they might see beauty, to open their ears that they might hear truth, to heal the brokenhearted and to make the sick whole. He calls us to do the same.

CARING MATTERS MOST

The giving of time is like the gift of money. Few and worthwhile contributions are better than many and meaningless ones. Where a woman makes this contribution will be the result of her own experience and concern. The difficulty is not in finding a place of need but in choosing a particular road of service on the large map of life. Life can become simplified as we grow in maturity—simple in the sense that desire for fashionableness, prestige, possessions may be whittled down; at the same time life becomes infinitely complex in regard to the number of calls upon one's time and energy. A deeply committed woman said recently to some of her younger friends, "You will learn, my dears, that the longer you live the more there is to do." Are we meant to be completely vulnerable, to feel an unlimited liability toward all who seem to need us? There is no easy answer. What one can and should do varies from year to year.

If we fail to keep the eternal rhythm between the "immeasurable world of being" and the "measurable world of doing" all our ceaseless activity will be a kind of running away from taking time to seek God at the center of life. The woman who is on every committee, every charitable organization, who rushes from this to that, always arriving breathless, is a familiar sight. Her activity is almost useless, bolstering only her own demanding ego. Somewhere between spreading ourselves too thin and doing nothing is a line of balance, a golden mean. The woman who learns the art of saying no and yes at the right times is learning to "mind her measure." And perhaps we bear always the "discipline of uncertainty" as to whether our decisions have been wise.

"The world is so seriously in need of mature, selfless people to set its problems to rights, people who will roll up their sleeves and work with love and imagination, people who will sit patiently on committees and find the creative answers. So many fine projects have been upset because someone's ego became a disintegrating factor! It is hard to be both arduous and objective at the same time."[2]

It is often far better to serve a few individuals than to try to ameliorate conditions for a multitude. In a book about Schweitzer and his work at Lambaréné, there is a picture of the good doctor sitting by a sick old African. "Did you sleep well?" "No," retorts the old patient, "I kept waiting for you to say good night."[3] It was Schweitzer's custom to make the rounds of the hospital wards every night, but some emergency kept him away that evening.

Before we sign ourselves up for an hour or a day each week, or each month, we need to be quite certain that nothing less than an emergency will keep us away from the place we have promised to be. For a shut-in or a convalescent who is counting on his new friend to read to him or write a letter or minister through the healing touch of strong soothing hands on a tired, aching back, to look forward to such a joy and to be forgotten is indeed a sore disappointment.

It is a sad fact that volunteers have a bad reputation. Unless every effort is bent toward being regular and dependable, it is better not to begin. It is not just some club that will be disappointed; it will be Mrs. Tucker, Mr. Broder, Mrs. Rhodes, Mr. Auten, Mr. McKeever, Miss Fowlen—individuals with whom we have identified ourselves, who will

---

2 *Toward a Less Divided Life* by Julia Lee Rubel, p. 18. Women's Problems Group of the Society of Friends. Used by permission.

3 *The World of Albert Schweitzer* by Erica Anderson and Eugene Exman. Harper and Brothers, 1955.

feel forsaken. "Caring," says von Huegel, "is most important, and caring is always costing." The curse of our machine culture is that people have lost their faces and become known as a lonely crowd. We are called to love people as individuals, to rescue them from the sea of mass anonymity, to save them from being thought of as just another case.

Richard Cabot began denouncing the sociologists' habit of treating people as cases as long ago as 1914. He would have approved Thomas Kelly's saying that "Social concern is the dynamic Life of God at work in the world, . . . particularized in each individual or group who is sensitive and tender in the leading-strings of love."[4]

The greatest gift of the volunteer worker is her willingness to know her new friends as individuals, to let them feel her respect and affection. Because the volunteer works with fewer people she has time to listen, time to be considerate over small problems that the overworked staff person busy with too many people, too many records, too many telephone calls, cannot manage. Because the professional social worker is already burdened she may not look with favor on the extra work entailed in the training of one more volunteer whose enthusiasm she considers may be a passing whim. Therefore, the volunteer may in the beginning become discouraged by being assigned what she evaluates as "busy work," piddling tasks of no importance. She may feel tied by red tape and bureaucratic methods. If she can weather her apprenticeship and prove her worth, her great contribution will lie in her willingness to take time for small services, to be endlessly patient over one person's troubles, to help carry out with sympathetic understanding the ideas of her new friends. Amateur service, small things done for love

---

[4] *A Testament of Devotion* by Thomas R. Kelly, p. 111. Harper and Brothers, 1941. Used by permission.

and with imagination, is "the dynamic life of God at work in the world."

WHO GIVES HIMSELF FEEDS THREE

The wonder of God's creation increases as one's own life is multiplied by personal identification with people of all ages and walks of life, as well as with all races and cultures. On every road new insights are gained. I learn about courtesy and cheerfulness from my poets at the Center for Older People. I learned about kindness from the girls in the county jail. "Mary, aren't your shoes too big?" "Yes'm, but I bought that size so my sister could wear them too." When the girls were working on small garments for the babies in Germany, it was explained that Sally was having a baby and maybe she needed the nighties and kimonos. I said, "Sally, you and Mary and Lois have done the sewing, you decide where they are most needed." Without a minute's hesitation, Sally said, "I want them to go to the little babies we heard about, the ones that are sometimes wrapped in newspapers. I'll have plenty of time to get things together for my baby when I get out of here."

In giving even a fragment of time and energy in personal ministry, one's own life is enriched a thousandfold. You may go to give of yourself as you read to a blind student, but end by receiving a new field of interest in the book read, a new and companionable friend, and an uplift to the soul from the example of his cheerful courage.

The satisfactions of the volunteer worker are countless. That does not mean the jobs are easy; it is because they present a challenge that they can be rewarding. A Companion of the Holy Cross has written: "Joy is an active partnership in redemptive effort, an energy of tense and urgent consecration. There is pain in it and uttermost agony, without which the joy would be incomplete."

The volunteer worker has taken her part in redemptive love; in serving her brother man she has served God; she has widened the road on which she travels until never again can life be monotonous, or boring, or empty, or lonely; she has diminished her own self-centeredness in helping to save the self-respect of others. She is on the way toward being a true follower of the Lord Jesus who, in the words of Russell Maltby, requires his disciples to be "absurdly happy, entirely fearless, and always in the midst of trouble."

The level of life on which women spend most of their time serving humanity, that horizontal bar of the cross which at first seemed to point in opposite directions, turns out to be all one piece, with no separation between work and family —between one's own and mankind. Carry the image a step further and picture that cross bar as the arms of Jesus who in his life on earth used them to encircle little children, to gather in the lonely, the guilty, the fearful, the rebellious, the despairing; gathering them in that they might know the love of their heavenly Father.

> If love should count you worthy, and should deign
> One day to seek your door and be your guest,
> Pause, ere you draw the bolt and bid him rest,
> If in your old content you would remain,
> For not alone he enters. In his train
> Are angels of the mist, the lonely guest,
> Dreams of the unfulfilled and unpossessed
> And sorrow, and life's immemorial pain!
> He wakes in you desires you never may forget.
> He shows you stars you never saw before.
> He makes you share with him, forevermore,
> The burden of the world's divine regret.
> How wise were you to open not, and yet
> How poor if you should turn him from the door!
>
> —*Sidney Lysaght*

+

7. *The Life of
     the Spirit*

THE CROSS is a symbol of "both and," not "either or." The
vertical bar represents not only the pull between earth and
heaven but the bond that holds them together. The horizontal bar unites work and relatedness, personal creation
and creative service to others.

As a violin cannot be played without the strings being
taut, so life cannot be lived at its best without tension between nature and spirit. When perfectly attuned, a life is
filled with harmony, even as music is brought forth from
wood and catgut if the tension is exact. Perhaps Christ—his
spirit of love and light, of truth and beauty—is the violin bow
waiting to bring the divine touch.

The cross becomes a plus sign pulling us together. For
the kingdom of heaven is within us earthborn creatures, and
nothing can separate us mortals from God and his love. But
we must become our best selves, having a fulfilled, useful,
creative self, in order to lose it in the lives of others. The
cross is the symbol of wholeness as well as holiness.

SOLITUDE

The temptation for most people is to live on the horizontal
plane of work and people. But the true original within each
of us can seldom evolve amid a constant pressure of outer

stimuli. We are so afraid of emptiness and nonbeing that we lack the courage to throw ourselves at the foot of the cross, or to seek the oversoul in its upward reaches. The peril of the modern woman is that she fails to take time to let her personality grow through solitude that gives pause for the development of the self through creating, imagining, loving, listening inwardly. Time to daydream, time to sit enfolded in peaceable greenness intent on the liquid song of a wood thrush, can germinate new life and make her whole.

The healing power of silence is nowhere better described, to my way of thinking, than in Mary Webb's *Precious Bane*. (This is one of those novels, I have heard women say, that changed their lives.)

And I ran away into the attic and cried a long while. But the quiet of the place, and the loneliness of it comforted me at long last, and I opened the shutter that gave on the orchard. . . .

The attic was close under the thatch, and there were many nests beneath the eaves, and a continual twittering of swallows . . . among the beams . . . was a wild bees' nest, and you could hear them making a sleepy soft murmuring. . . . So, it being very still there, with the fair shadows of the apple trees peopling the orchard outside, . . . there came to me, I cannot tell whence, a most powerful sweetness that had never come to me afore. It was not religious, like the goodness of a text heard at a preaching. It was beyond that. It was as if some creature made all of light had come on a sudden from a great way off, and nestled in my bosom. On all things there came a fair, lovely look, as if a different air stood over them. . . .

And it was as wilful in its coming and going as a breeze over the standing corn. It was a queer thing, too, that a woman who spent her days in sacking, cleaning sties and beast-housen, living hard, . . . should come of a sudden into such a marvel as this. For though it was so quiet, it was a great miracle, and it changed my life; for when I was lost for something to turn to, I'd run to the attic, and it was a core of sweetness in much bitter.

Though the visitation came but seldom, the taste of it was in the attic all the while. I had but to creep in there, and hear the bees making their murmur, and smell the woody, o'er-sweet scent of kept apples, and hear the leaves rasping softly on the window-frame, and watch the twisted grey twigs on the sky, and I'd remember it and forget all else. . . .

I fell to thinking how all this blessedness of the attic came through me being curst. For if I hadna had a hare-lip to frighten me away into my own lonesome soul, this would never have come to me. The apples would have crowded all in vain to see a marvel, for I should never have known the glory that came from the other side of silence.

Even while I was thinking this, out of nowhere suddenly came that lovely thing, and nestled in my heart, like a seed from the core of love.[1]

NURTURE OF THE SPIRIT AT NIGHT

Is there perhaps a relation between such quiet wakeful musing and the healing refreshment that comes in sleep? In the right amount of sleep, that is, for there is a golden mean between "sleeping ourselves stupid" and burning the candle at both ends. George Macdonald has a theory that I like: In relaxed sleep not only does the tired body become rested and, being rested, freshens the mind; but of more importance, in sleep the soul goes home to God, and there being close to the Heart of Creation, returns creative and bouyant. The quickening of the spirit in sleep energizes the body and likewise sets free the mind. That is why the early waking hours should be used for creative work and prayer; the soul is freshly returned from the Creator.

Ideas come in sleep; solutions to problems come up out

---

[1] *Precious Bane* by Mary Webb, pp. 61-64. Jonathan Cape, 1928.

of the unconscious if sleep is trusted as a period of spiritual activity as well as a time of physical restoration. A famous author once told how an assignment came to her that seemed to be beyond her powers. She went to sleep with complete trust that her need could be put into God's hands. On awaking, she took pencil and paper and wrote out without further change the article requested.

The mystics have always thought well of sleep; at least Brother Lawrence gives such encouragement: "Those who have the gale of the Holy Spirit go forward, even in sleep." And many authorities write of the importance of prayer as one settles to sleep and then again in the first waking moments. Perhaps the night prayers should be simple trusting ones. Mother Currier suggests that we give God back the day, saying, "Thou knowest, Lord." The way in which we say farewell to the soul as it slips into sleep is as important as how we say farewell to a child departing for school, or the atmosphere in which a husband is sent off to work. (It is common knowledge that accidents multiply when a member of the family is sent off in anger or despair.) So with ourselves —the waking thoughts are largely governed by those with which the soul is sent to sleep.

Word pictures, the great collects, psalms of praise and thanksgiving, soothe and bless the subliminal mind in this realm of drifting between the unconscious and the conscious world. Simple repetitive prayers and psalms are best, like "Take not thy Holy Spirit from us" and "The Lord is my Shepherd," or perhaps singsong verses such as these by Fray Angelico Chavez:

> When cares at night
> Keep me from sleep
> In my mind's eye
> I count my sheep.

And as I scan
Their passing by,
I spy a man
Who watches nigh.

A Shepherd he
Of gentle charms:
A lamb I see
Within his arms.

He looks at me
I look at him
Till sheep and he
Grow misty dim.

Thus sure I am
To sleep and rest
Just like the lamb
Upon his breast.[2]

If sleeplessness comes it need not be restlessness and rebellion at wakefulness. It can be a kind of creative acceptance. How should the person of faith use the wakeful periods in the middle of the night?

Long before I knew what it was not to go to sleep the minute my head touched the pillow, my farmer neighbor told me that often in the night he had wakeful times when he repeated to himself all the psalms he had learned as a boy. After awhile he would go to sleep and find he was just as rested in the morning as if it had been solid sleep.

A beloved older Friend of our Meeting was an invalid suffering excruciating pain her last several years. Yet when we went to see her she was always cheerful. She would tell

---

2 "Shepherds" by Fray Angelico Chavez in *From the Good Treasure of Companions, Far and Near.*

of the long night vigils: traveling in memory to places of great beauty, or recalling one by one her schoolteachers, or remembering events connected with each Christmas holiday. Always she seemed filled to overflowing with thanksgiving for the richness of her days. She knew well that that which you have in your heart can never be taken from you.

Closely related to the recollection of pleasant memories as a means of nurturing the spiritual life at night is the saying over to oneself passages of great poetry. It is well to feed the subconscious with great rhythms of beauty and hope, with belief in growth, and with the longing in each of us for perfection. I often turn to Masefield and Blake, and especially to Evelyn Underhill's "Theophany":

> Deep-cradled in the fringed mow to lie
> And feel the rhythmic flux of life sweep by,
> This is to know the easy heaven that waits
> Before our timidly-embattled gates:
> To share the exultant leap and thrust of things
> Outward toward perfection, in the heart
> Of every bud to see the folded wings,
> Discern the patient Whole in every part.[3]

If after an hour or two of poetry and prayer I am still wide awake, I usually get up and make use of this gift of silent hours for some creative work. At three o'clock in the morning the mind is especially active. Many people have said that the early dawn is the most fruitful, fertile time of all the twenty-four hours. Revelations that seem filled with truth and beauty keep pushing for expression. They may be the very same insights that have come on many other occasions, but each time they come with newness of life. Whether or not there comes inspiration for a poem, it can

---

[3] *Immanence: A Book of Verses* by Evelyn Underhill, p. 35. E. P. Dutton and Company, 1912. Used by permission.

be a fine time for writing letters. Or the creative reading that gets crowded aside in a busy day may now be enjoyed. My day is not spoiled after such a wide-awake night. A nap of twenty or thirty minutes in the afternoon seems to take the place of two or three hours at night. If a midday nap cannot be managed, I am quite certain to have a sound sleep the following night. The important thing is to accept with cheerfulness whichever comes, sound sleep or creative wakefulness, even wakefulness that is forced upon us.

A friend wrote me how she learned to pray, and how her youngest son has kept her growing in the life of the spirit. "There was a time in my life when for various reasons I decided I was through with God and prayer. Then when Paul was nine years old, Mark was born, and I decided that God was good after all, and prayer a fine thing and I would do some. But I was not allowed to make my own terms with God. For over two years Mark got me up at night, not once or twice, but five or six times! And God would say, 'You can pray now, Blanche.' I was never able to find any other reason for Mark's extreme wakefulness. You do think God has a sense of humor, don't you? Now that he is nine, our rebellious, obstreperous, acutely sensitive Mark continues to call me to worship in many ways."

WHOLENESS

A wise physician has said that every doctor knows that sleep, change, love, and light are the four healers. I like to remember that the word health comes from the same source as hale, whole, holy. Sleep is a return to the Godhead when we may go forward with the gale of the Holy Spirit. Sleep is necessary and no one can be in good health without some measure of rest produced by sleep. But to some degree, change and love and light can take the place of sleep.

Change, in order to be healing, need not be geographical.

It may rather be change of pace, of occupation, or attitude of mind. A mind that is turned toward God in gratitude for his grace so freely bestowed, that is fed on beautiful poetry, that reaches out through prayer in loving embrace of God's children, is made whole through that change of direction as truly as if it had returned through sleep to the Creator.

Without love, neither body nor spirit can ever be whole. Health of body, wholeness of mind, holiness of spirit are deeply related. Love is essential to each. This I deeply believe. And yet there is a mystery about the nature of healing and suffering that I do not comprehend, even while glimpsing the spiritual validity of both. I am convinced that Jesus cured incurables. I am convinced that there have been miraculous recoveries at Lourdes. Yet, why are not all healed? It does not seem to rest upon the faith of the sick person.

Why did so many of the saints suffer grievous physical afflictions? Paul had his thorn in the flesh, Francis his blindness and ravishing diseases, Teresa her morning sickness and constant discomfort. Sometimes the only prayer that can be made is one that is wrung out of suffering: "Lord, take this pain; it is the only gift I have to give."

Healing of the physical body may or may not come to pass. The thing that matters is that the spirit be made whole, open to God's love, tender to all his creation. The important thing is that we find a faith by which to live, whether with bodily well-being or with nagging pain; and a faith by which to die, so that we know that nothing—neither sickness nor health—can separate us from the love of God.

Light is the most difficult of the four healers for the physician to prescribe. Yet oddly enough how a person sleeps, or does not sleep, is of tremendous consequence in his ability to find the light. Light is the most important of the four healing qualities, for it is light in which each soul must live and move and have its being if the body is to be a temple of the living God. Growth into the light can come in the darkness of the night as well as in the sunshine of the day, can come in the dark night of the soul, in the blackness of despair. All growth is nurtured in darkness, the seed in the good earth, the bird in the egg, the child in the womb. But there is no further growth if the soul, or the seed, or the bird, or the child, stays incased in its shell of darkness. If we go to bed in quiet trust that the Heart of the Eternal is carrying us toward the light, even as the earth is turning with us toward the sun, it matters little whether we actually sleep, or whether we simply rest in the assurance of God's restoring love and light.

PRAYER

As we return again to the idea of the cross as a sign post, let us think of the vertical bar stretching upward toward Divine Light, to God's gracious love, to the practice of worship and prayer. If the cross is rooted in the good earth, representing one kind of recreation, the figure of speech must be continued to include the upward striving by which the ego is at last transcended. Exposure to light is necessary for growth and fullness of life unless we are content to molder away in a mushroom-like existence. The light and love of God need to shine on good things like hoeing gardens and playing chess and having babies, or those good things which seemed worthwhile may become boring, monotonous, and purposeless. To recognize the light the practice of prayer is necessary to most of us.

A voice speaking to me and to many of my friends is that of Florence Allshorn. Only an excerpt can be given here, but I recommend J. H. Oldham's biography of her. She encourages me because she believes it possible to grow in the life of the spirit through practice.

The only way I can learn it is to do it, and one thing I am very sure of for myself is that to sit quietly before God doing nothing, only fixing the will gently on some expressive word like "O God, I want thee" or "Father" or "Here am I and here are you" makes a world of difference. Just as lying in the sun doing nothing, surrendering your body to it, with the sun blazing down on you, affects your body and your senses, so this surrendering of the soul to that transforming Power affects the soul, and I believe that as truly as the sun changes the color of your skin so that Power changes you at the center.[4]

But must everyone consciously practice the presence of God in order to become whole? Some, I believe, do not. A few rare souls from babyhood on, seem singularly sweet and completely whole in all parts of their being. They are those who live with a sense of wonder, with a delight in beauty and goodness, with a kindly affection and friendliness for all creation. They are living in God, and God shines forth through them. They have their feet on the "Ground of all Being" and their eyes are set on the everlasting hills.

Some blessed few never lose this childlike faith and acceptance of the wonder of creation and their responsibility for its continuing good order. But most of us fall from such a state of grace and then through what is called prayer strive to rediscover God. When conscious communication begins to be sought, it may take the form of intellectual questioning, of theological debating, or of working through a kind of adolescent rebellion, before simple childlike communion is again established with the Father.

If this were not the supreme attitude in prayer, Jesus would not have reminded his followers again and again of their need of becoming like children. He would not have told the parable of a loving Father longing for his prodigal

---

[4] *Florence Allshorn* by J. H. Oldham, p. 141. Harper and Brothers. Used by permission of Student Christian Movement Press, Ltd.

children to return to his encompassing heart. Even as a parent of many children loves each child's differing characteristics—the one dreamy and poetic, the one practical and always seeing a job to do and a way to complete it, one impetuous and stubborn—so the heavenly Father loves us at whatever stage we are, whichever path we have stumblingly taken toward him. And if we fall, he cares; for not one sparrow shall fall without his caring. We are not promised that the sparrow shall not fall, but that God cares whatever happens.

Probably most people turn to God and pray for his help out of extreme despair rather than from philosophical searching. Even as a lost child discovers its forsaken state and cries out for its parent, so is the prayer of need wrung out of those at the end of their own resources. Intense pain, primeval grief, or a facing up to sin brings out the desperate plea, "O God, O God, help me now, this is more than I can bear." It is praying not as we would, but as we must. God hears us where we are and delivers us from the evil that has cut us off from his presence.

Likewise, there is a prayer for others that is involuntary. Spontaneous prayer for others wells up regardless of any will to do so, out of pure affection or deep concern. Knowing that your friend is going through some crisis you find him involuntarily again and again in your consciousness; you then have the choice of fearing that the worst will come to pass, or, if you are a person of prayer, of helping to hold him above the deep waters toward the Light, the Source of all healing and redemption.

Thanksgiving and Intercession

When his faith was at its lowest point, G. K. Chesterton tells us that it was preserved by his gratitude toward God: "I hung on to religion by one thin thread of thanks."

Another authority on the life of the spirit has said that every day we should begin our prayers with thanksgiving. We should thank God for our bodies which are the temple of the Holy Spirit. We should thank God for the wish to know him, for the desire and longing to be certain of his merciful love. And we should thank God for our friends: those who love us when we err, who make his existence real when our own spirits are bogged in darkness and doubt and despair.

Gratitude to God may be very elementary prayer, but an acknowledgment of our blessings is surely a step further than merely petitioning him for personal favors. Having found a company of the holy, perhaps the safest practice is to let our friends pray for us while we intercede for them. Phillips Brooks, Forbes Robinson, so many have said they could do more for a man in an hour of prayer than in any other form of ministry.

The following letter from a friend is an illustration of the awareness of such a need: "God surely works in ways beyond us to teach us the truths he is trying to show; we must see them for ourselves, difficult as that may be. I am working steadily and there is much I have to be grateful for. The Prophet said, 'Much in you is still man, and much in you is not yet man, but a shapeless pigmy that walks asleep in the mist searching for its own awakening.'[5] Those are good lines for me. We who are legion need the prayers of you who have faith."

It would seem that important as are the kindly deeds of neighbors and volunteers, the encouraging words of counselors and friends, the greatest ministry one person can give another is the gift of prayer. George Buttrick answers the questions that clamor within us.

---

[5] Gibran, *op. cit.,* p. 46. Used by permission.

"But does God rest my neighbor's good on prayers?" we may ask, shrinking from the burden of so great an obligation. Why should we doubt that God imposes such a burden of love? The responsibility is stern and splendid. God rests our neighbor's good upon our toil and thought. Why not upon our prayers? "But would not God give good gifts in any event?" Apparently there are some gifts which God chooses to give through love's labor and planning—and prayer. God is intent upon the growth of the comradeship. . . . He yearns to see "The Beloved Community" fulfilled on earth. Therefore he has made us one life. We must not fail those whose weal depends upon our toil and thought—and prayer.[6]

In George Macdonald's novel *Sir Gibbie* there is old Janet, a mother whose heart was so wide she was always collecting those who needed a bit of mothering. When she prayed, she never said she was praying for people, but that she was keeping them company, and holding the gate open. Janet was a true follower of our Lord, holding the gate open that Christ's love might break through to our hard hearts, making us tender and affectionate to each other.

With the growing sense of being members one of another, intercessory prayer becomes as important as feeding those who hunger and clothing the naked. My friend in Wales who was the wife of a Baptist minister once wrote, "However much one loves people it is my experience that one can skip their needs from one's mind unless reminded by a list on paper. It is a good discipline and helps to make their needs alive in my heart and mind." She went on to tell of an old gardener who always spoke of the "Communion Service as Christ's own forget-me-not." The members of our meditation group have little handmade booklets in which are clipped the prayers we love and the names of people for whom we all

---

[6] *Prayer* by George A. Buttrick, p. 112. Abingdon Press, 1942. Used by permission.

mean to intercede. For instance: "Almighty and everlasting God, who art always more ready to hear than we to pray, and art wont to give more than either we desire or deserve; grant us so to know thee that we may truly love thee, and so to love thee that we may become channels for thy love to reach——." "May the tenderness and warmth of thy unconquerable love fill all the hurt, bruised, fearful places in ——'s spirit and release in him thy security and gladness and peace." "Dear Lord, since thou art the Vine and —— is a branch, he is rooted and grounded in love. Thy redemptive love can make him whole." Our friends carry us and we carry them and so through prayer are we "laced together."

An awareness of our interdependence became vivid to me one evening as a friend and I sat before the fire puzzling over the hands clasped in prayer in a picture of Rodin's "The Cathedral." My guest said, "I have tried and tried to put my hands into that position and simply cannot." Never before having noticed anything incomprehensible about these beautiful sculptured hands, now I too made an attempt. Suddenly, the two of us reached out to each other, and placing our right hands together formed such a handclasp as that in the great work of art. It takes the creative love of two individuals caring for each other and reaching up to God in their togetherness to break down man's separate pride and build the Cathedral of Prayer.

As we continue to seek the life of the spirit we begin to see how love is at the heart of the cross, how love is the lodestar by which we set our pace no matter whether it carry us earthward, or outward, or upward. Through experience we have learned that love is both immanent and transcendent.

Recollection

We are to be childlike, Jesus taught, and to love one another, if we would be his disciples. Beyond that he said the essence of prayer was to be found in withdrawal from crowds of people and from pressures of business. "Come ye apart." As the demands and responsibilities and concerns of modern life increase, the more imperative to set aside a regular time to "wait for the Lord." The invisible world of the Spirit has a way of becoming dim when things and people and deadlines crowd in on every waking moment. Perspective will return as we are still and cool in mind and soul. It takes solitude and serenity to contemplate whatsoever is true and beautiful and just and pure and of good report. Today, we all believe this. It does not take the courage now that it did in the sophisticated twenties to say, "I have a daily period of meditation," or "Pray for me," but it still takes discipline and an act of will to save an hour or even ten minutes to come directly into the presence of God and let his light and lovingkindness fill our spirits.

Whether a devotional book, memorized prayers, great poetry, scriptural reading, contemplative silence, is relied upon does not matter. There are as many ways to feed the soul as there are ways to feed the body. And perhaps *when* we pray does not matter either—the dog does very well on one meal a day, the rabbit nibbles continuously.

> In the castle of my soul
> Is a little postern gate,
> Where, when I enter,
> I am in the presence of God.
> In a moment, in the turning of a thought,
> I am where God is.
>
> When I enter into God
> All life has meaning.

Without asking I know,
My desires are even now fulfilled,
My fever is gone
In the great quiet of God,
My troubles are but the pebbles on the road,
My joys are like the everlasting hills.
So it is when I step through the gate of prayer
From time into eternity.
So it is when my soul slips through the
    postern gate
Into the presence of God.
Big things become small, and small things
    become great.
The near becomes far, and the future near.
The lowly and despised is shot through
    with glory.
When I am in him, I am in the kingdom of
    God
And in the Fatherhood of my soul.

                              —*Walter Rauschenbusch*

Jesus told simple little stories for our nurture. If we become sufficiently childlike we can take his words literally: "Come to me, all who labor and are heavy-laden, and I will give you rest. Take my yoke upon you, and learn from me; for I am gentle and lowly in heart, and you will find rest for your souls. For my yoke is easy, and my burden is light." If we take the yoke it means that of our own free will we walk tethered to Christ. Never again shall we face trouble or grief or pain or joy alone. If our will is one with his will of lovingkindness, then we shall be bound to him with gladness; then we shall walk yoked with him in sweet content and grateful humility. His spirit of love and light and truth is a constant companion. His presence is closer than hands and feet. He gives rest and renewal to our souls. He bears our burdens with us. His mercy endureth forever.